ZEN

IN THE

ART

OF

WRITING

ZEN
IN THE
ART
OF
WRITING

RAY BRADBURY

BANTAM BOOKS
NEW YORK • TORONTO • LONDON • SYDNEY • AUCKLAND

ZEN IN THE ART OF WRITING

*A Bantam Book / published by arrangement with
Capra Press*
BANTAM NONFICTION *and the portrayal of a boxed "b" are
trademarks of Bantam Books, a division of Bantam Doubleday Dell
Publishing Group, Inc.*

*PRINTING HISTORY
Capra Press edition published 1990
Bantam edition / April 1992*

ISBN 0-553-29634-5

Published simultaneously in the United States and Canada

*Bantam Books are published by Bantam Books, a division of Bantam
Doubleday Dell Publishing Group, Inc. Its trademark, consisting of the
words "Bantam Books" and the portrayal of a rooster, is Registered in U.S.
Patent and Trademark Office and in other countries. Marca Registrada.
Bantam Books, 666 Fifth Avenue, New York, New York 10103.*

PRINTED IN THE UNITED STATES OF AMERICA

OPM   0 9 8 7 6 5 4 3 2 1

TO MY FINEST TEACHER,
JENNET JOHNSON,
WITH LOVE

CONTENTS

CONTENTS

HOW TO CLIMB THE TREE OF LIFE, THROW ROCKS AT YOURSELF, AND GET DOWN AGAIN WITHOUT BREAKING YOUR BONES OR YOUR SPIRIT

A PREFACE WITH A TITLE NOT MUCH LONGER THAN THE BOOK

Sometimes I am stunned at my capacity as a nine-year-old, to understand my entrapment and escape it.

How is it that the boy I was in October, 1929, could, because of the criticism of his fourth-grade schoolmates, tear up his Buck Rogers comic strips and a month later judge all of his friends idiots and rush back to collecting?

Where did that judgment and strength come from? What sort of process did I experience to enable me to say: I am as good as dead. Who is killing me? What do I suffer from? What's the cure?

I was able, obviously, to answer all of the above. I named the sickness: my tearing up the strips. I found the cure: go back to collecting, no matter what.

I did. And was made well.

But still. At *that* age? When we are accustomed to responding to peer pressure?

Where did I find the courage to rebel, change my life, live alone?

I don't want to over-estimate all this, but damn it, I love that nine-year-old, whoever in hell he was. Without him, I could not have survived to introduce these essays.

Part of the answer, of course, is in the fact that I was so madly in love with Buck Rogers, I could not see my love, my hero, my life, destroyed. It is almost that simple. It was like having your best all-round greatest-loving-buddy, pal, center-of-life drown or get shot-gun killed. Friends, so killed, cannot be saved from funerals. Buck Rogers, I realized, might know a second life, if I gave it to him. So I breathed in his mouth and, lo!, he sat up and talked and said, what?

Yell. Jump. Play. Out-run those sons-of-bitches. They'll *never* live the way you live. Go *do* it.

Except I never used the S.O.B. words. They were not allowed. Heck! was about the size and strength of my outcry. *Stay alive!*

So I collected comics, fell in love with carnivals and World's Fairs and began to write. And what, you ask, does writing teach us?

First and foremost, it reminds us that we *are* alive and that it is gift and a privilege, not a right. We must earn life once it has been awarded us. Life asks for rewards back because it has favored us with animation.

So while our art cannot, as we wish it could, save us from wars, privation, envy, greed, old age, or death, it can revitalize us amidst it all.

Second, writing is survival. Any art, *any* good work, of course, is that.

Not to write, for many of us, is to die.

We must take arms each and every day, perhaps knowing that the battle cannot be entirely won, but fight we must, if only a gentle bout. The smallest effort to win means, at the end of each day, a sort of victory. Remember that pianist who said that if he did not practice every day *he* would know, if he did not practice for two days, the *critics* would know, after three days, his *audiences* would know.

A variation of this is true for writers. Not that your style, whatever that is, would melt out of shape in those few days.

But what would happen is that the world would catch up with and try to sicken you. If you did not write every day, the poisons would accumulate and you would begin to die, or act crazy, or both.

You must stay drunk on writing so reality cannot destroy you.

For writing allows just the proper recipes of truth, life, reality as you are able to eat, drink, and digest without hyperventilating and flopping like a dead fish in your bed.

I have learned, on my journeys, that if I let a day go by without writing, I grow uneasy. Two days and I am in tremor. Three and I suspect lunacy. Four and I might as well be a hog, suffering the flux in a wallow. An hour's writing is tonic. I'm on my feet, running in circles, and yelling for a clean pair of spats.

So *that*, in one way or another, is what this book is all about.

Taking your pinch of arsenic every morn so you can survive to sunset. Another pinch at sunset so that you can more-than-survive until dawn.

The micro-arsenic-dose swallowed here prepares you *not* to be poisoned and destroyed up ahead.

Work in the midst of life is that dosage. To manipulate life, toss the bright-colored orbs up to mix with the dark ones, blending a variation of truths. We use the grand and beautiful facts of existence in order to put up with the horrors that afflict us directly in our families and friends, or through the newspapers and TV.

The horrors are not to be denied. Who amongst us has not had a cancer-dead friend? Which family exists where some relative has not been killed or maimed by the automobile? I know of none. In my own circle, an aunt, and uncle, and a cousin, as well as six friends, have been destroyed by the car. The list is endless and crushing if we do not creatively oppose it.

Which means writing as cure. Not completely, of course. You never get over your parents in the hospital or your best love in the grave.

I won't use the word "therapy," it's too clean, too sterile a word. I only say when death slows others, you must leap to set up your diving board and dive head first into your typewriter.

The poets and artists of other years, long past, knew all and everything I have said here, or put in the following essays. Aristotle said it for the ages. Have you listened to him lately?

These essays were written at various times over a thirty-year period, to express special discoveries, to serve special needs. But they all echo the same truths of explosive self-revelation and continuous astonishment at what your deep well contains if you just haul off and shout down it.

Even as I write this, a letter has come from a young, unknown writer, who says he is going to live by my motto, found in my *Toynbee Convector*.

". . . to gently lie and prove the lie true . . . everything is finally a promise . . . what *seems* a lie is a ramshackle need, wishing to be born. . . ."

And now:

I have come up with a new simile to describe myself lately. It can be yours.

Every morning I jump out of bed and step on a landmine. The landmine is me.

After the explosion, I spend the rest of the day putting the pieces together.

Now, it's your turn. Jump!

ACKNOWLEDGMENTS

The essays in this collection orginally appeared in the following publications, to whose editors and publishers thanks are due

"The Joy of Writing," *Zen & the Art of Writing, Capra Chapbook Thirteen*, Capra Press, 1973.

"Run Fast, Stand Still, or, The Thing at the Top of the Stairs, or, New Ghosts from Old Minds," *How to Write Tales of Horror, Fantasy & Science Fiction*, edited by J.A. Williamson, Writers Digest Books, 1986.

"How to Keep and Feed a Muse," *The Writer*, July, 1961.

"Drunk, and in Charge of a Bicycle," An introduction to *The Collected Stories of Ray Bradbury*, Alfred A. Knopf, Inc., 1980.

"Investing Dimes: *Fahrenheit 451*," An introduction to *Fahrenheit 451*, Limited Editions Club, 1982.

"Just This Side of Byzantium: Dandelion Wine," An introduction to *Dandelion Wine*, Alfred A. Knopf, Inc., 1974.

ACKNOWLEDGMENTS

"On the Shoulders of Giants. . . ." Originally published as the Preface to *Other Worlds: Fantasy and Science Fiction Since 1939*, edited by John J. Teunissen, University of Manitoba Press, 1980. Reprinted in Special Issue of *MOSAIC*, XIII/3-4(Spring-Summer, 1980).

"The Secret Mind," *The Writer*, November, 1965.

"Zen in the Art of Writing," *Zen & the Art of Writing, Capra Chapbook Thirteen*, Capra Press, 1973.

THE JOY OF WRITING

Zest. Gusto. How rarely one hears these words used. How rarely do we see people living, or for that matter, creating by them. Yet if I were asked to name the most important items in a writer's make-up, the things that shape his material and rush him along the road to where he wants to go, I could only warn him to look to his zest, see to his gusto.

You have your list of favorite writers; I have mine. Dickens, Twain, Wolfe, Peacock, Shaw, Molière, Jonson, Wycherly, Sam Johnson. Poets: Gerard Manley Hopkins, Dylan Thomas, Pope. Painters: El Greco, Tintoretto. Musicians: Mozart, Haydn, Ravel, Johann Strauss(!). Think of all these names and you think of big or little, but nonetheless important, zests, appetites, hungers. Think of Shakespeare and Melville and you think of thunder, lightning, wind. They all knew the joy of creating in large or small forms, on unlimited or restricted canvasses. These are the children of the gods. They knew fun in their work. No matter if creation came hard here and there along the way, or what illnesses and tragedies touched their most private lives. The important things are those passed down to us from their hands and minds and these are full to bursting with animal vigor and intellectual vitality. Their hatreds and despairs were reported with a kind of love.

Look at El Greco's elongation and tell me, if you can, that he had no joy in his work? Can you really pretend that Tintoretto's *God Creating the Animals of the Universe* is a work founded on anything less than "fun" in its widest and most completely involved sense? The best Jazz says, "Gonna live forever; don't believe in death."

The best sculpture, like the head of Nefertiti, says again and again, "The Beautiful One was here, is here, and will be here, forever." Each of the men I have listed seized a bit of the quicksilver of life, froze it for all time and turned, in the blaze of their creativity, to point at it and cry, "Isn't this good!" And it was good.

What has all this to do with writing the short story in our times?

Only this: if you are writing without zest, without gusto, without love, without fun, you are only half a writer. It means you are so busy keeping one eye on the commercial market, or one ear peeled for the avant-garde coterie, that you are not being yourself. You don't even know yourself. For the first thing a writer should be is—excited. He should be a thing of fevers and enthusiasms. Without such vigor, he might as well be out picking peaches or digging ditches; God knows it'd be better for his health.

How long has it been since you wrote a story where your real love or your real hatred somehow got onto the paper? When was the last time you dared release a cherished prejudice so it slammed the page like a lightning bolt? What are the best things and the worst things in your life, and when are you going to get around to whispering or shouting them?

Wouldn't it be wonderful, for instance, to throw down a copy of *Harper's Bazaar* you happened to be leafing through at the dentist's, and leap to your typewriter and ride off with hilarious anger, attacking their silly and sometimes shocking snobbishness? Years ago I did just that. I came across an issue where the *Bazaar* photographers, with their perverted sense of equality, once again utilized natives in a Puerto Rican backstreet as props in front of which their starved-looking mannikins postured for the benefit of yet more emaciated half-women in the best salons in the country. The photographs so enraged me I ran, did not walk, to my machine and wrote "Sun and Shadow," the story of an old Puerto Rican who ruins the *Bazaar* photographer's afternoon by sneaking into each picture and dropping his pants.

I dare say there are a few of you who would like to have done this job. I had the fun of doing it; the cleansing aftereffects of the hoot, the holler, and the great horselaugh. Probably the editors at the *Bazaar* never heard. But a lot of readers did and cried, "Go it,

Bazaar, go it, Bradbury!" I claim no victory. But there was blood on my gloves when I hung them up.

When was the last time you did a story like that, out of pure indignation?

When was the last time you were stopped by the police in your neighborhood because you like to walk, and perhaps think, at night? It happened to me just often enough that, irritated, I wrote "The Pedestrian," a story of a time, fifty years from now, when a man is arrested and taken off for clinical study because he insists on looking at un-televised reality, and breathing un-air-conditioned air.

Irritations and angers aside, what about loves? What do you love most in the world? The big and little things, I mean. A trolley car, a pair of tennis shoes? These, at one time when we were children, were invested with magic for us. During the past year I've published one story about a boy's last ride in a trolley that smells of all the thunderstorms in time, full of cool—green moss-velvet seats and blue electricity, but doomed to be replaced by the more prosaic, more practical-smelling bus. Another story concerned a boy who wanted to own a pair of new tennis shoes for the power they gave him to leap rivers and houses and streets, and even bushes, sidewalks, and dogs. The shoes were to him, the surge of antelope and gazelle on African summer veldt. The energy of unleashed rivers and summer storms lay in the shoes;

he had to have them more than anything else in the world.

So, simply then, here is my formula.

What do you want more than anything else in the world? What do you love, or what do you hate?

Find a character, like yourself, who will want something or not want something, with all his heart. Give him running orders. Shoot him off. Then follow as fast as you can go. The character, in his great love, or hate, will rush you through to the end of the story. The zest and gusto of his need, and there *is* zest in hate as well as in love, will fire the landscape and raise the temperature of your typewriter thirty degrees.

All of this is primarily directed to the writer who has already learned his trade; that is, has put into himself enough grammatical tools and literary knowledge so he won't trip himself up when he wants to run. The advice holds good for the beginner, too, however, even though his steps may falter for purely technical reasons. Even here, passion often saves the day.

The history of each story, then, should read almost like a weather report: Hot today, cool tomorrow. This afternoon, burn down the house. Tomorrow, pour cold critical water upon the simmering coals. Time enough to think and cut and rewrite tomorrow. But today—explode—fly apart—disintegrate! The other six or seven drafts are going to be pure torture. So why not enjoy the first draft, in the hope that your joy will seek and find others in the world who, reading your story, will catch fire, too?

It doesn't have to be a big fire. A small blaze, candlelight perhaps; a longing for a mechanical wonder like a trolley or an animal wonder like a pair of sneakers rabbiting the lawns of early morning. Look for the little loves, find and shape the little bitternesses. Savor them in your mouth, try them on your typewriter. When did you last read a book of poetry or take time, of an afternoon, for an essay or two? Have you ever read a single issue of *Geriatrics*, the Official Journal of the American Geriatrics Society, a magazine devoted to "research and clinical study of the diseases and processes of the aged and aging"? Or read, or even seen, a copy of *What's New*, a magazine published by the Abbott Laboratories in North Chicago, containing articles such as "Tubocurarene for Cesarean Section" or "Phenurone in Epilepsy," but also utilizing poems by William Carlos Williams, Archibald Macleish, stories by Clifton Fadiman and Leo Rosten; covers and interior illustrations by John Groth, Aaron Bohrod, William Sharp, Russell Cowles? Absurd? Perhaps. But ideas lie everywhere, like apples fallen and melting in the grass for lack of wayfaring strangers with an eye and a tongue for beauty, whether absurd, horrific, or genteel.

Gerard Manley Hopkins put it this way:

Glory be to God for dappled things—
For skies of couple-color as a brinded cow;
For rose-moles all in stipple upon trout that
swim;
Fresh-firecoal chestnut-falls; finches' wings;
Landscape plotted and pieced—fold, fallow, and
plow;
And all trades, their gear and tackle and trim.
All things counter, original, spare, strange;
Whatever is fickle, freckled (who knows how?)
With swift, slow; sweet, sour; adazzle, dim;
He fathers-forth whose beauty is past change:
Praise Him.

Tom Wolfe ate the world and vomited lava. Dickens dined at a different table every hour of his life. Molière, tasting society, turned to pick up his scalpel, as did Pope and Shaw. Everywhere you look in the literary cosmos, the great ones are busy loving and hating. Have you given up this primary business as obsolete in your own writing? What fun you are missing, then. The fun of anger and disillusion, the fun of loving and being loved, of moving and being moved by this masked ball which dances us from cradle to churchyard. Life is short, misery sure, mortality certain. But on the way, in your work, why not carry those two inflated pig-bladders labeled Zest and Gusto. With them, traveling to the grave, I intend to slap some dummox's behind, pat a pretty girl's coiffure, wave to a tad up a persimmon tree.

Anyone wants to join me, there's plenty of room in Coxie's Army.

1973

RUN FAST, STAND

STILL, OR, THE THING

AT THE TOP OF THE

STAIRS, OR, NEW

GHOSTS FROM OLD

MINDS

Run fast, stand still. This, the lesson from lizards. For all writers. Observe almost any survival creature, you see the same. Jump, run, freeze. In the ability to flick like an eyelash, crack like a whip, vanish like steam, here this instant, gone the next—life teems the earth. And when that life is not rushing to escape, it is playing statues to do the same. See the hummingbird, there, not there. As thought arises and blinks off, so this thing of summer vapor; the clearing of a cosmic throat, the fall of a leaf. And where it was—a whisper.

What can we writers learn from lizards, lift from birds? In quickness is truth. The faster you blurt, the more swiftly you write, the more honest you are. In hesitation is thought. In delay comes the effort for a style, instead of leaping upon truth which is the *only* style worth deadfalling or tiger-trapping.

In between the scurries and flights, what? Be a chameleon, ink-blend, chromosome change with the landscape. Be a pet rock, lie with the dust, rest in the rainwater in the filled barrel by the drainspout outside your grandparents' window long ago. Be dandelion wine in the ketchup bottle capped and placed with an inked inscription: June morn, first day of Summer, 1923. Summer 1926, Fireworks Night. 1927: Last Day of Summer. LAST OF THE DANDELIONS, Oct. 1st.

And out of all this, wind up with your first success as a writer, at $20 a story, in *Weird Tales*.

How *do* you commence to start to begin an almost new kind of writing, to terrify and scare?

You stumble into it, mostly. You don't know what you're doing, and suddenly, it's done. You don't set out to reform a certain kind of writing. It evolves out of your own life and night scares. Suddenly you look around and see that you have done something almost fresh.

The problem for any writer in any field is being circumscribed by what has gone before or what is being printed that very day in books and magazines.

I grew up reading and loving the traditional ghost stories of Dickens, Lovecraft, Poe, and later, Kuttner, Bloch, and Clark Ashton Smith. I tried to write stories heavily influenced by various of these writers, and succeeded in making quadruple-layered mudpies, all language and style, that would not float, and sank without a trace. I was too young to identify my problem, I was so busy imitating.

I almost blundered into my creative self in my last year in high school, when I wrote a kind of long remembrance of the deep ravine in my home town, and my fear of it at night. But I had no story to go with the ravine, so my discovering the true source of my future writing was put off for some few years.

I wrote at least a thousand words a day every day from the age of twelve on. For years Poe was looking over one shoulder, while Wells, Burroughs, and just about every writer in *Astounding* and *Weird Tales* looked over the other.

I loved them, and they smothered me. I hadn't learned how to look away and in the process look not at myself but at what went on behind my face.

It was only when I began to discover the treats and tricks that came with word association that I began to find some true way through the minefields of imitation. I finally figured out that if you are going to step on a live mine, make it your own. Be blown up, as it were, by your *own* delights and despairs.

I began to put down brief notes and descriptions of loves and hates. All during my twentieth and twenty-first years, I circled around summer noons and October midnights, sensing that there somewhere in the bright and dark seasons must be something that was really me.

I finally found it one afternoon when I was twenty-two years old. I wrote the title "The Lake" on the first page of a story that finished itself two hours later. Two hours after that I was sitting at my typewriter out on a porch in the sun, with tears running off the tip of my nose, and the hair on my neck standing up.

Why the arousal of hair and the dripping nose?

I realized I had at last written a really fine story. The first, in ten years of writing. And not only was it a fine story, but it was some sort of hybrid, something verging on the new. Not a traditional ghost story at all, but a story about love, time, remembrance, and drowning.

I sent it off to Julie Schwartz, my pulp agent, who liked it, but said it was not a traditional tale and might be hard to sell. *Weird Tales* walked around it, touched it with a ten-foot pole, and finally decided, what the hey, to publish it, even though it didn't fit their magazine. But I must promise, next time, to write a good old-fashioned ghost story! I promised. They gave me twenty dollars, and everyone was happy.

Well, some of you know the rest. "The Lake" has been reprinted dozens of times in the forty-four years since. And it was the story that first got various editors of other magazines to sit up and notice the guy with the aroused hair and the wet nose.

Did I learn a hard, fast, or even an easy lesson from "The Lake"? I did not. I went back to writing the old-fashioned ghost story. For I was far too young to understand much about writing at all, and my discoveries went unnoticed by me for years. I was wandering all over the place and writing poorly much of the time.

During my early twenties, if my weird fiction was imitative, with an occasional surprise of a concept and a further surprise in execution, my science–fiction writing was abysmal, and my detective fiction verged on the ludicrous. I was deeply under the influence of my loving friend, Leigh Brackett, whom I used to meet every Sunday at Muscle Beach in Santa Monica, California, there to read her superior Stark on Mars tales, or to envy and try to emulate her *Flynn's Detective* stories.

But along through those years I began to make lists of titles, to put down long lines of *nouns*. These lists were the provocations, finally, that caused my better stuff to surface. I was feeling my way toward something honest, hidden under the trapdoor on the top of my skull.

The list ran something like this:

THE LAKE. THE NIGHT. THE CRICKETS. THE RAVINE. THE ATTIC. THE BASEMENT. THE TRAPDOOR. THE BABY. THE CROWD. THE NIGHT TRAIN. THE FOG HORN. THE SCYTHE. THE CARNIVAL. THE CAROUSEL. THE DWARF. THE MIRROR MAZE. THE SKELETON.

I was beginning to see a pattern in the list, in these words that I had simply flung forth on paper, trusting my subconscious to give bread, as it were, to the birds.

Glancing over the list, I discovered my old love and fright having to do with circuses and carnivals. I remembered, and then forgot, and then remembered again, how terrified I had been when my mother took me for my first ride on a merry-go-round. With the calliope screaming and the world spinning and the terrible horses leaping, I added my shrieks to the din. I did not go near the carousel again for years. When I really did, decades later, it rode me into the midst of *Something Wicked This Way Comes*.

But long before that, I went on making the lists. THE MEADOW. THE TOY CHEST. THE MONSTER. TYRANNOSAURUS REX. THE TOWN CLOCK. THE OLD MAN. THE OLD WOMAN. THE TELEPHONE. THE SIDEWALKS. THE COFFIN. THE ELECTRIC CHAIR. THE MAGICIAN.

Out on the margin of these nouns, I blundered into a science-fiction story that was not a science-fiction story. My title was "R is for Rocket." The published title was "King of the Grey Spaces," the story of two boys, great friends, one elected to go off to the Space Academy, the other staying home. The tale was rejected by every science-fiction magazine because, after all, it was only a story about friendship being tested by circumstance, even though the circumstance was space travel. Mary Gnaedinger, at *Famous Fantastic Mysteries*, took one look at my story and published it. But, again, I was too young to see that "R is for Rocket" would be the kind of story that would make me as a science-fiction writer, admired by some, and criticized by many who observed that I was no writer of science fiction, I was a "people" writer, and to hell with that!

I went on making lists, having to do not only with night, nightmares, darkness, and objects in attics, but the toys that men play with in space, and the ideas I found in detective magazines. Most of the detective material I published in my twenty-fourth year in *Detective Tales* and *Dime Detective* is not worth rereading. Here and there, I fell over my own shoelaces and did a nearly good job of remembering Mexico, which scared me, or downtown Los Angeles during the Pachucho riots. But is would take me the better part of forty years to assimilate the detective/mystery/suspense genre and make it work for me in my latest novel, *Death Is a Lonely Business*.

But back to my lists. And *why* go back to them? Where am I leading you? Well, if you are a writer, or would hope to be one, similar lists, dredged out of the lopside of your brain, might well help you discover *you*, even as I flopped around and finally found me.

I began to run through those lists, pick a noun, and then sit down to write a long prose-poem-essay on it.

Somewhere along about the middle of the page, or perhaps on the second page, the prose poem would turn into a story. Which is to say that a character suddenly appeared and said, "That's *me*"; or, "That's an idea *I like!*" And the character would then finish the tale for me.

It began to be obvious that I was learning from my lists of nouns, and that I was further learning that my *characters* would do my work *for* me, if I let them alone, if I gave them their heads, which is to say, their fantasies, their frights.

I looked at my list, saw SKELETON, and remembered the first artworks of my childhood. I drew skeletons to scare my girl cousins. I was fascinated with those unclothed medical displays of skulls and ribs and pelvic sculptures. My favorite tune was "'Tain't No Sin, To Take Off Your Skin, and Dance Around in Your Bones."

Remembering my early artwork and my favorite tune, I ambled into my doctor's office one day with a sore throat. I touched my Adam's apple, and the tendons on each side of my neck, and asked for his medical advice.

"Know what you're suffering from?" asked the doc.

"What?"

"*Discovery* of the larynx!" he crowed. "Take some aspirin. Two dollars, please!"

Discovery of the larynx! My God, how *beautiful*! I trotted home, feeling my throat, and then my ribs, and then my medulla oblongata, and my kneecaps.

Holy Moses! Why not write a story about a man who is terrified to discover that under his skin, inside his flesh, *hidden*, is a symbol of all the Gothic horrors in history—a skeleton!

The story wrote itself in a few hours.

A perfectly obvious concept, yet no one else in the history of writing weird tales had ever scribbled it down. I fell into my typewriter with it and came up with a brand-new, absolutely original tale, which had been lurking under my skin since I first drew a skull and crossbones, aged six.

I began to gain steam. The ideas came faster now, and all of them from my lists. I prowled up in my grandparents' attics and down in their basements. I listened to the middle-of-the-night locomotives wailing across the northern Illinois landscape, and that was death, a funeral train, taking my loved ones away to some far graveyard. I remembered five o'clock in the morning, pre-dawn arrivals of Ringling Brothers, Barnum and Bailey, and all the animals parading by before sunrise, heading for the empty meadows where the great tents would rise like incredible mushrooms. I remembered Mr. Electrico and his traveling electric chair. I remembered Blackstone the Magician dancing magical handkerchiefs and vanishing elephants on my hometown stage. I remembered my grandfather, my sister, and various aunts and cousins, in the coffins and gone forever in the tombyards where the butterflies settled like flowers on the graves and where the flowers blew away like butterflies over the stones. I remembered my dog, lost for days, coming home late on a winter night with snow and mud and leaves in his pelt. And the stories began to burst, to explode from those memories, hidden in the nouns, lost in the lists.

My remembrance of my dog, and his winter pelt, became "The Emissary," the story of a boy, sick in bed, who sends his dog out to gather the seasons in his fur, and report back. And then, one night, the dog comes back from a journey to the graveyard, and brings "company" with him.

My listed title THE OLD WOMAN became two stories, one "There Was an Old Woman," about a lady who refused to die and demands her body back from the undertakers, defying Death, and a second tale, "Season of Disbelief," about some children who refuse to believe that a very old woman was ever young, was ever a girl, a child. The first story appeared in my first collection, *Dark Carnival*. The second became part of a further word-association test I gave myself, called *Dandelion Wine*.

We can surely see now, can't we, that it is the personal observation, the odd fancy, the strange conceit, that pays off. I was fascinated by old people. I tried to solve their mystery with my eyes and young mind but was continually astounded to realize that once upon a time they had been me, and some day up ahead I would be them. Absolutely impossible! Yet there the boys and girls were, locked in old bodies, a dreadful situation, a terrible trick, right before my gaze.

Pilfering from my list, again, I seized out the title THE JAR, the result of my being stunned at an encounter with a series of embryos on display in a carnival when I was twelve and again when I was fourteen. In those long-gone days of 1932 and 1934, we children knew nothing, of course, absolutely nothing about sex and procreation. So you can imagine how astounded I was when I prowled through a free carnival exhibit and saw all those fetuses of humans and cats and dogs, displayed in labeled jars. I was shocked by the look of the unborn dead, and the new mysteries of life they caused to rise up in my head later that night and all through the years. I never mentioned the jars and the formaldehyde fetuses to my parents. I knew I had stumbled on some truths which were better not discussed.

All of this surfaced, of course, when I wrote "The Jar," and the carnival and the fetal displays and all the old terrors poured out of my fingertips into my typewriter. The old mystery had finally found a resting place, in a story.

I found another title in my list, THE CROWD. And, typing furiously, I recalled a terrible collision when I was fifteen and ran from a friend's house at the sound, to be confronted by a car that had hit an obstruction in the street and rocketed into a telephone pole. The car was split in half. Two people lay dead on the pavement, another woman died just as I reached her, her face ruined. Another man died a minute later. Still another died the next day.

I had never seen anything like it. I walked home, bumping into trees, in shock. It took me months to get over the horror of that scene.

Years later, with my list before me, I remembered a number of peculiar things about that night. The accident had occurred at an intersection surrounded on one side by empty factories and a deserted school-yard, and on the opposite side, by a graveyard. I had come running from the nearest house, a hundred yards away. Yet, within moments, it seemed, a crowd had gathered. Where had they all come from? Later on in time, I could only imagine that some came, in some strange fashion, out of the empty factories, or even more strangely, out of the graveyard. After typing for only a few minutes, it came to me that, yes, this crowd was *always* the same crowd, that it gathered at *all* accidents. These were victims from accidents years ago, doomed to come back and haunt the scene of new accidents as they occurred.

Once I hit on this idea, the story finished itself in a single afternoon.

Meanwhile, the carnival artifacts were gathering closer, their great bones starting to thrust up through my skin. I was making longer and longer prose poem excursions about circuses that arrived long after midnight. During those years, in my early twenties, prowling a Mirror Maze on the old Venice Pier with my friends Leigh Brackett and Edmond Hamilton, Ed suddenly cried, "Let's get out of here, before Ray writes a story about a dwarf who pays his way in here every night so he can stand and make himself tall in the big stretch mirror!" "That's it!" I shouted, and ran home to write "The Dwarf." "That'll teach me to shoot off my mouth," said Ed, when he read the story the next week.

THE BABY on that list was, of course, me.

I remembered an old nightmare. It was about being born. I remembered lying in my crib, three days old, wailing with the knowledge of being thrust out into the world; the pressure, the cold, the shrieking into life. I remembered my mother's breast. I remembered the doctor, on the fourth day of my life, bending over me with a scalpel to perform circumcision. I remembered, I remembered.

I changed the title from THE BABY to "The Small Assassin." That story has been anthologized dozens of times. And I had lived the story, or part of it, from my first hour of life onward, and only truly remembered and nailed it down in my twenties.

Did I write stories based on every single noun in my pages and pages of lists?

Not all. But most. THE TRAP DOOR, listed way back in 1942 or '43, didn't surface until three years ago, as a story in *Omni*.

Another story about me and my dog took more than fifty years to surface. In "Bless Me, Father, for I Have Sinned," I went back in time to relive a beating I had given my dog when I was twelve, and for which I had never forgiven myself. I wrote the story to at last examine that cruel, sad boy and put his ghost, and the ghost of my much-loved dog, to rest forever. It was the same dog, incidentally, who brought "company" back from the graveyard in *The Emissary*.

During these years, Henry Kuttner, along with Leigh, was my teacher. He suggested authors—Katherine Anne Porter, John Collier, Eudora Welty—and books—*The Lost Weekend, One Man's Meat, Rain in the Doorway*—to be read and learned from. Along the way, he gave me a copy of *Winesburg, Ohio*, by Sherwood Anderson. Finishing the book, I said to myself, "Someday I would like to write a novel laid on the planet Mars, with somewhat similar people." I immediately jotted down a list of the sorts of folks I would want to plant on Mars, to see what would happen.

I forgot *Winesburg, Ohio* and my list. Over the years,

I wrote a series of stories about the Red Planet. One day, I looked up and the book was finished, the list complete, *The Martian Chronicles* on its way to publication.

So there you have it. In sum, a series of nouns, some with rare adjectives, which described a territory unknown, an undiscovered country, part of it Death, the rest Life. If I had not made up these prescriptions for Discovery I would never have become the jackdaw archaeologist or anthropologist that I am. That jackdaw who seeks bright objects, odd carapaces and misshapen femurs from the boneheaps of junk inside my head, where lay strewn the remnants of collisions with life as well as Buck Rogers, Tarzan, John Carter, Quasimodo, and all the other creatures who made me want to live forever.

In the words of the old Mikado song, I had a little list, save it was a long one, which led me into Dandelion Wine country and helped me move the Dandelion Wine country up to Mars, and ricocheted me back into dark wine territory as Mr. Dark's night train arrived long before dawn. But the first and most important pileup of nouns was the one filled with leaves whispering along the sidewalks at 3:00 A.M. and funerals wheeling by on empty railtracks, following, and crickets that suddenly, for no reason, shut up, so you could hear your own heart, and wish you couldn't.

Which leads us to a final revelation—

One of the nouns on my list in high school was THE THING, or, better yet, THE THING AT THE TOP OF THE STAIRS.

When I was growing up in Waukegan, Illinois, there was only one bathroom; upstairs. You had to climb an unlit hall halfway before you could find and turn on a light. I tried to get my dad to keep the light on all night. But that was expensive stuff. The light stayed off.

Around two or three in the morning, I would have to go to the bathroom. I would lie in bed for half an hour or so, torn between the agonized need for relief, and what I knew was waiting for me in the dark hall leading up to the attic. At last, driven by pain, I would edge out of our dining room into that hall, thinking: run fast, leap up, turn on the light, but whatever you do, don't look up. If you look up before you get the light on, *It* will be there. The Thing. The terrible Thing waiting at the top of the stairs. So run, blind; don't look.

I ran, I leaped. But always, I couldn't help it, at the last moment, I blinked and stared into the awful darkness. And it was always there. And I screamed and fell back downstairs, waking my parents. My dad would groan and turn over in bed, wondering where this son of his had come from. My mother would get up, find me in a scrambled heap in the hall, and go up to turn on the light. She would wait for me to climb up to the bathroom and come back down to have my tearstained face kissed and my terrified body tucked in bed.

The next night and the next night and the night after that, the same thing happened. Driven mad by my hysterics, Dad got out the old chamber pot and shoved it under my bed.

But I was never cured. The Thing remained there forever. Only moving West when I was thirteen got me away from that terror.

What have I done, recently, about that nightmare? Well . . .

Now, very late in time, The Thing is standing up at the top of the stairs, still waiting. From 1926 to now, in the spring of 1986, is a long waiting. But at last, gleaning my ever dependable list, I have typed the noun out on paper, added "The Stairs," and I have finally faced up to the dark climb and the Arctic coldness held in place for sixty years, waiting to be asked to come down through my frozen fingertips and into your bloodstream. The story, associated out of memory, was finished this week, even as I wrote this essay.

I leave you now at the bottom of your own stair, at half after midnight, with a pad, a pen, and a list to be made. Conjure the nouns, alert the secret self, taste the darkness. You own Thing stands waiting 'way up there in the attic shadows. If you speak softly, and write any old word that wants to jump out of your nerves onto the page . . .

Your Thing at the top of your stairs in your own private night . . . may well come *down*.

1986

HOW TO KEEP AND

FEED A MUSE

It isn't easy. Nobody has ever done it consistently. Those who try hardest, scare it off into the woods. Those who turn their backs and saunter along, whistling softly between their teeth, hear it treading quietly behind them, lured by a carefully acquired disdain.

We are of course speaking of The Muse.

The term has fallen out of the language in our time. More often than not when we hear it now we smile and summon up images of some fragile Greek goddess, dressed in ferns, harp in hand, stroking the brow of your perspiring Scribe.

The Muse, then, is that most terrified of all the virgins. She starts if she hears a sound, pales if you ask her questions, spins and vanishes if you disturb her dress.

What ails her? you ask. Why does she flinch at the stare? Where does she come from and where go? How can we get her to visit for longer periods of time? What temperature pleasures her? Does she like loud voices, or soft? Where do you buy food for her, and of what quality and quantity, and what hours for dining?

We might start off by paraphrasing Oscar Wilde's poem, substituting the word "Art" for "Love."

Art will fly if held too lightly,
Art will die if held too tightly,
Lightly, tightly, how do I know
Whether I'm holding or letting Art go?

For "Art" substitute, if you wish, "Creativity" or "The Subconscious" or "Heat" or whatever your own word is for what happens when you spin like a firewheel and a story "happens."

Another way of describing The Muse might be to reassess those little specks of light, those airy bubbles which float across everyone's vision, minute flaws in the lens or the outer, transparent skin of the eye. Unnoticed for years, when you first focus your attention on them, they can become unbearable nuisances, ruptures in one's attention at all hours of the day. They spoil what you are looking at, by getting in the way. People have gone to psychiatrists with the problem of "specks." The inevitable advice: ignore them, and they'll go away. The fact is, they don't go away; they remain, but we focus out beyond them, on the world and the world's ever-changing objects, as we should.

So, too, with our Muse. If we focus beyond her, she regains her poise, and stands out of the way.

It is my contention that in order to Keep a Muse, you must first offer food. How you can feed something that isn't yet there is a little hard to explain. But we live surrounded by paradoxes. One more shouldn't hurt us.

The fact is simple enough. Through a lifetime, by ingesting food and water, we build cells, we grow, we become larger and more substantial. That which was not, *is*. The process is undetectable. It can be viewed only at intervals along the way. We know it is happening, but we don't know quite how or why.

Similarly, in a lifetime, we stuff ourselves with sounds, sights, smells, tastes, and textures of people, animals, landscapes, events, large and small. We stuff ourselves with these impressions and experiences and our reaction to them. Into our subconscious go not only factual data but reactive data, our movement toward or away from the sensed events.

These are the stuffs, the foods, on which The Muse grows. This is the storehouse, the file, to which we must return every waking hour to check reality against memory, and in sleep to check memory against memory, which means ghost against ghost, in order to exorcise them, if necessary.

What is The Subconscious to every other man, in its creative aspect becomes, for writers, The Muse. They are two names for one thing. But no matter what we call it, here is the core of the individual we pretend to extol, to whom we build shrines and hold lip-services in our democratic society. Here is the stuff of originality. For it is in the totality of experience reckoned with, filed, and forgotten, that each man is truly different from all others in the world. For no man sees the same events in the same order, in his life. One man sees death younger than another, one man knows love more quickly than another. Two men, as we know, seeing the same accident, file it with different cross-references, in another part of their own alien alphabet. There are not one-hundred elements, but two billion elements in the world. All would assay differently in the spectroscopes and scales.

We know how fresh and original is each man, even the slowest and dullest. If we come at him right, talk him along, and give him his head, and at last say, What do you want? (Or if the man is very old, What *did* you want?) every man will speak his dream. And when a man talks from his heart, in his moment of truth, he speaks poetry.

I have had this happen not once but a thousand times in my life. My father and I were really not great friends, until very late. His language, his thought, from day to day, were not remarkable, but whenever I said, "Dad, tell me about Tombstone when you were seventeen," or "the wheatfields, Minnesota, when you were twenty," Dad would begin to speak about running away from home when he was sixteen, heading west in the early part of this century, before the last boundaries were fixed—when there were no highways, only horse paths, and train tracks, and the Gold Rush was on in Nevada.

Not in the first minute, or the second, or the third minute, no, did the thing happen to Dad's voice, did the right cadence come, or the right words. But after he had talked five or six minutes and got his pipe going, quite suddenly the old passion was back, the old days, the old tunes, the weather, the look of the sun, the sound of the voices, the boxcars traveling late at night, the jails, the tracks narrowing to golden dust behind, as the West opened up before—all, all of it, and the cadence there, the moment, the many moments of truth, and, therefore, poetry.

The Muse was suddenly there for Dad.

The Truth lay easy in his mind.

The Subconscious lay saying its say, untouched, and flowing off his tongue.

As we must learn to do in our writing.

As we can learn from every man or woman or child around us when, touched and moved, they tell of something they loved or hated this day, yesterday, or some other day long past. At a given moment, the fuse, after sputtering wetly, flares, and the fireworks begin.

Oh, it's limping crude hard work for many, with language in their way. But I have heard farmers tell about their very first wheat crop on their first farm after moving from another state, and if it wasn't Robert Frost talking, it was his cousin, five times removed. I have heard locomotive engineers talk

ZEN IN THE ART OF WRITING

about America in the tones of Tom Wolfe who rode our country with his style as they ride it in their steel. I have heard mothers tell of the long night with their firstborn when they were afraid that they and the baby might die. And I have heard my grandmother speak of her first ball when she was seventeen. And they were all, when their souls grew warm, poets.

If it seems I've come the long way around, perhaps I have. But I wanted to show what we all have in us, that it has always been there, and so few of us bother to notice. When people ask me where I get my ideas, I laugh. How strange—we're so busy looking out, to find ways and means, we forget to look *in*.

The Muse, to belabor the point then, is there, a fantastic storehouse, our complete being. All that is most original lies waiting for us to summon it forth. And yet we know it is not as easy as that. We know how fragile is the pattern woven by our fathers or uncles or friends, who can have their moment destroyed by a wrong word, a slammed door, or a passing fire-wagon. So, too, embarrassment, self-consciousness, remembered criticisms, can stifle the average person so that less and less in his lifetime can he open himself out.

Let's say that each of us has fed himself on life, first, and later, on books and magazines. The difference is that one set of events happened to us, and the other was forced feeding.

If we are going to diet our subconscious, how prepare the menu?

Well, we might start our list like this:

Read poetry every day of your life. Poetry is good because it flexes muscles you don't use often enough. Poetry expands the senses and keeps them in prime condition. It keeps you aware of your nose, your eye, your ear, your tongue, your hand. And, above all, poetry is compacted metaphor or simile. Such metaphors, like Japanese paper flowers, may expand outward into gigantic shapes. Ideas lie everywhere through the poetry books, yet how rarely have I heard short story teachers recommending them for browsing.

My story, "The Shoreline at Sunset," is a direct result of reading Robert Hillyer's lovely poem about finding a mermaid near Plymouth Rock. My story, "There Will Come Soft Rains," is based on the poem of that title by Sara Teasdale, and the body of the story encompasses the theme of her poem. From Byron's, "And the Moon Be Still as Bright," came a chapter for my novel *The Martian Chronicles*, which speaks for a dead race of Martians who will no longer prowl empty seas late at night. In these cases, and dozens of others, I have had a metaphor jump at me, give me a spin, and run me off to do a story.

What poetry? Any poetry that makes your hair stand up along your arms. Don't force yourself too hard.

Take it easy. Over the years you may catch up to, move even with, and pass T. S. Eliot on your way to other pastures. You say you don't understand Dylan Thomas? Yes, but your ganglion does, and your secret wits, and all your unborn children. Read him, as you can read a horse with your eyes, set free and charging over an endless green meadow on a windy day.

What else fits in our diet?

Books of essays. Here again, pick and choose, amble along the centuries. You'll have much to pick over from the days before the essay became less popular. You can never tell when you might want to know the finer points of being a pedestrian, keeping bees, carving headstones, or rolling hoops. Here is where you play the dilettante, and where it pays to do so. You are, in effect, dropping stones down a well. Every time you hear an echo from your Subconscious, you know yourself a little better. A small echo may start an idea. A big echo may result in a story.

In your reading, find books to improve your color sense, your sense of shape and size in the world. Why not learn about the senses of smell and hearing? Your characters must sometimes use their noses and ears or they may miss half the smells and sounds of the city, and all of the sounds of the wilderness still loose in the trees and on the lawns of the city.

Why all this insistence on the senses? Because in

order to convince your reader that he is *there*, you must assault each of his senses, in turn, with color, sound, taste, and texture. If your reader feels the sun on his flesh, the wind fluttering his shirt sleeves, half your fight is won. The most improbable tales can be made believable, if your reader, through his senses, feels certain that he stands at the middle of events. He cannot refuse, then, to participate. The logic of events always gives way to the logic of the senses. Unless, of course, you do something really unforgivable to wrench the reader out of context, such as having the American Revolution won with machine guns, or introducing dinosaurs and cave men into the same scene (they lived millions of years apart). Even with this last, a well-described, technically perfect Time Machine can suspend disbelief again.

Poetry, essays. What about short stories, novels? Of course. Read those authors who write the way you hope to write, those who think the way you would like to think. But also read those who do not think as you think or write as you want to write, and so be stimulated in directions you might not take for many years. Here again, don't let the snobbery of others prevent you from reading Kipling, say, while no one else is reading him.

Ours is a culture and a time immensely rich in trash as it is in treasures. Sometimes it is a little hard to tell the trash from the treasure, so we hold back, afraid to declare ourselves. But since we are out to give ourselves texture, to collect truths on many levels, and in many ways, to test ourselves against life, and the truths of others, offered us in comic strips, TV shows, books, magazines, newspapers, plays, and films, we should not fear to be seen in strange companies. I have always felt on good terms with Al Capp's "Lil Abner." I think there is much to be learned about child psychology from "Peanuts." A whole world of romantic adventure has existed, beautifully drawn by Hal Foster in his "Prince Valiant." As a boy I collected and was perhaps influenced in my later books by the wonderful middle-class American daily strip "Out Our Way" by J. C. Williams. I am as much Charlie Chaplin in *Modern Times* in 1935 as I am Aldous Huxley's reader-friend in 1961. I am not one thing. I am many things that America has been in my time. I had enough sense to keep moving, learning, growing. And I have never reviled or turned my back on the things I grew out of. I learned from Tom Swift, and I learned from George Orwell. I delighted in Edgar Rice Burroughs's *Tarzan* (and still respect that old delight and will not be brainwashed from it) as today I delight in C. S. Lewis's *Screwtape Letters*. I have known Bertrand Russell and I have known Tom Mix, and my Muse has grown out of the mulch of good, bad, and indifferent. I am such a creature as can remember with love not only Michelangelo's Vatican ceilings but the long-gone sounds of the radio show, "Vic and Sade."

What is the pattern that holds all this together? If I have fed my Muse on equal parts of trash and treasure, how have I come out at the farther end of life with what some people take to be acceptable stories?

I believe one thing holds it all together. Everything I've ever done was done with excitement, because I wanted to do it, because I loved doing it. The greatest man in the world for me, one day, was Lon Chaney, was Orson Welles in *Citizen Kane*, was Laurence Olivier in *Richard III*. The men change, but one thing remains always the same: the fever, the ardor, the delight. Because I wanted to do, I did. Where I wanted to feed, I fed. I remember wandering, stunned, off a stage in my home town, holding a live rabbit given to me by Blackstone the Magician in the greatest performance ever! I remember wandering, stunned, in the papier-mâché streets of the Century of Progress Exhibition in Chicago in 1933; in the halls of the Venetian doges in Italy in 1954. The quality of each event was immensely different, but my ability to drink it in, the same.

This does not mean to say that one's reaction to everything at a given time should be similar. First off, it cannot be. At ten, Jules Verne is accepted, Huxley rejected. At eighteen, Tom Wolfe accepted, and Buck

Rogers left behind. At thirty, Melville discovered, and Tom Wolfe lost.

The constant remains: the search, the finding, the admiration, the love, the honest response to materials at hand, no matter how shabby they one day seem, when looked back on. I sent away for a statue of an African gorilla made of the cheapest ceramics when I was ten, said statue a reward for enclosing the wrapper from a package of Fould's Macaroni. The gorilla, arriving by mail, got a reception as large as that given the Boy David at his first unveiling.

The Feeding of the Muse then, which we have spent most of our time on here, seems to me to be the continual running after loves, the checking of these loves against one's present and future needs, the moving on from simple textures to more complex ones, from naïve ones to more informed ones, from nonintellectual to intellectual ones. Nothing is ever lost. If you have moved over vast territories and dared to love silly things, you will have learned even from the most primitive items collected and put aside in your life. From an ever-roaming curiosity in all the arts, from bad radio to good theatre, from nursery rhyme to symphony, from jungle compound to Kafka's *Castle*, there is basic excellence to be winnowed out, truths found, kept, savored, and used on some later day. To be a child of one's time is to do all these things.

Do not, for money, turn away from all the stuff you have collected in a lifetime.

Do not, for the vanity of intellectual publications, turn away from what you are—the material within you which makes you individual, and therefore indispensable to others.

To feed your Muse, then, you should always have been hungry about life since you were a child. If not, it is a little late to start. Better late than never, of course. Do you feel up to it?

It means you must still take long walks at night around your city or town, or walks in the country by day. And long walks, at any time, through bookstores and libraries.

And while feeding, How to *Keep* Your Muse is our final problem.

The Muse must have shape. You will write a thousand words a day for ten or twenty years in order to try to give it shape, to learn enough about grammar and story construction so that these become part of the Subconscious, without restraining or distorting the Muse.

By living well, by observing as you live, by reading well and observing as you read, you have fed Your Most Original Self. By training yourself in writing, by repetitious exercise, imitation, good example, you have made a clean, well-lighted place to keep the Muse. You have given her, him, it, or whatever, room to turn around in. And through training, you have relaxed yourself enough not to stare discourteously when inspiration comes into the room.

You have learned to go immediately to the typewriter and preserve the inspiration for all time by putting it on paper.

And you have learned the answer to the question asked earlier: Does creativity like loud or soft voices?

The loud, the passionate voice seems to please most. The voice upraised in conflict, the comparison of opposites. Sit at your typewriter, pick characters of various sorts, let them fly together in a great clang. In no time at all, your secret self is roused. We all like decision, declaration; anyone loudly for, anyone loudly against.

This is not to say the quiet story is excluded. One can be as excited and passionate about a quiet story as any. There is excitement in the calm still beauty of a *Venus de Milo*. The spectator, here, becomes as important as the thing viewed.

Be certain of this: When honest love speaks, when true admiration begins, when excitement rises, when hate curls like smoke, you need never doubt that creativity will stay with you for a lifetime. The core of your creativity should be the same as the core of your story and of the main character in your story. What does your character want, what is his dream, what shape has it, and how expressed? Given expression, this is the dynamo of his life, and your life, then, as Creator. At the exact moment when truth erupts, the subconscious changes from wastebasket file to angel writing in a book of gold.

Look at yourself then. Consider everything you have fed yourself over the years. Was it a banquet or a starvation diet?

Who are your friends? Do they believe in you? Or do they stunt your growth with ridicule and disbelief? If the latter, you haven't friends. Go find some.

And finally, have you trained well enough so you can say what you want to say without getting hamstrung? Have you written enough so that you are relaxed and can allow the truth to get out without being ruined by self-conscious posturings or changed by a desire to become rich?

To feed well is to grow. To work well and constantly is to keep what you have learned and know in prime condition. Experience. Labor. These are the twin sides of the coin which when spun is neither experience nor labor, but the moment of revelation. The coin, by optical illusion, becomes a round, bright, whirling globe of life. It is the moment when the porch swing creaks gentle and a voice speaks. All hold their breath. The voice rises and falls. Dad tells of other years. A ghost rises off his lips. The subconscious stirs and rubs its eyes. The Muse ventures in the ferns below the porch, where the summer boys, strewn on the lawn, listen. The words become poetry that no one minds, because no one has thought to call it that. Time is there. Love is there. Story is there. A well-fed man keeps and calmly gives forth his infinitesimal portion of eternity. It sounds big in the summer night. And it is, as it always was down the ages, when there was a man with something to tell, and ones, quiet and wise, to listen.

A CLOSING NOTE

"The first movie star I remember is Lon Chaney.

The first drawing I made was a skeleton.

The first awe I remember having was of the stars on a summer night in Illinois.

The first stories I read were science-fiction stories in *Amazing*.

The first time I ever went away from home was to go to New York and see the World of the Future enclosed in the Perisphere and shadowed by the Trylon.

My first decision about a career was at eleven, to be a magician and travel the world with my illusions.

My second decision was at twelve when I got a toy typewriter for Christmas.

And I decided to become a writer. And between the decision and the reality lay eight years of junior high school, high school, and selling newspapers on a street corner in Los Angeles, while I wrote three million words.

My first acceptance came from Rob Wagner's *Script* Magazine, when I was twenty.

My second sale was to *Thrilling Wonder Stories*.

My third was to *Weird Tales*.

Since then I have sold 250 stories to almost every magazine in the U.S., plus writing the screenplay of *Moby Dick* for John Huston.

I have written about the Lon Chaney-and-the-skeleton-people for *Weird Tales*.

I have written about Illinois and its wilderness in my *Dandelion Wine* novel.

I have written about those stars over Illinois, to which a new generation is going.

I have made worlds of the future on paper, much like that world I saw in New York at the Fair as a boy.

And I have decided, very late in the day, that I never gave up my first dream.

I am, like it or not, some sort of magician after all, half-brother to Houdini, rabbit-son of Blackstone, born in the cinema light of an old theatre, I would like to think (my middle name is Douglas; Fairbanks was at his height when I arrived in 1920), and matured at a perfect time—when man makes his last and greatest step out away from the sea that birthed him, the cave that sheltered him, the land that held him, and the air that summoned him so that he could never rest.

In sum, I am a piebald offspring of our mass-moved, mass-entertained, alone-in-a-New-Year's-crowd age.

It is a great age to live in and, if need be, die in and for. Any magician worth his salt would tell you the same."

1961

DRUNK, AND IN

CHARGE OF A BICYCLE

In 1953 I wrote an article for *The Nation* defending my work as a science-fiction writer, even though that label only applied to perhaps one third of my output each year.

A few weeks later, in late May, a letter arrived from Italy. On the back of the envelope, in a spidery hand, I read these words:

> B. Berenson
> I Tatti, Settignano
> Firenze, Italia

I turned to my wife and said, "My God, this can't be from *the* Berenson, can it, the great art historian?!"

"Open it," said my wife.

I did, and read:

Dear Mr. Bradbury:

In 89 years of life, this is the first fan letter I have written. It is to tell you that I have just read your article in *The Nation*—"Day After Tomorrow." It is the first time I have encountered the statement by an artist in any field, that to work creatively he must put flesh into it, and enjoy it as a lark, or as a fascinating adventure.

How different from the workers in the heavy industry that professional writing has become!

If you ever touch Florence, come to see me.

Sincerely yours. B. BERENSON.

Thus, at the age of thirty-three, I had my way of seeing, writing and living approved of by a man who became a second father to me.

I needed that approval. We all need someone higher, wiser, older to tell us we're not crazy after all, that what we're doing is all right. All right, hell, *fine*!

But it is easy to doubt yourself, because you look around at a community of notions held by other writers, other intellectuals, and they make you blush with guilt. Writing is supposed to be difficult, agonizing, a dreadful exercise, a terrible occupation.

But, you see, my stories have led me through my life. They shout, I follow. They run up and bite me on the leg—I respond by writing down everything that goes on during the bite. When I finish, the idea lets go, and runs off.

That is the kind of life I've had. Drunk, and in charge of a bicycle, as an Irish police report once put it. Drunk with life, that is, and not knowing where off to next. But you're on your way before dawn. And the trip? Exactly one half terror, exactly one half exhilaration.

When I was three my mother snuck me in and out of movies two or three times a week. My first film was Lon Chaney in *The Hunchback of Notre Dame*. I suffered permanent curvature of the spine *and* of my imagination that day a long time ago in 1923. From that hour on, I knew a kindred and wonderfully grotesque compatriot of the dark when I saw one. I ran off to see all the Chaney films again and again to be deliciously frightened. The Phantom of the Opera stood astride my life with his scarlet cape. And when it wasn't the Phantom it was the terrible hand that gestured from behind the bookcase in *The Cat and the Canary*, bidding me to come find more darkness hid in books.

I was in love, then, with monsters and skeletons and circuses and carnivals and dinosaurs and, at last, the red planet, Mars.

From these primitive bricks I have built a life and a career. By my staying in love with all of these amazing things, all of the good things in my existence have come about.

In other words, I was *not* embarrassed at circuses. Some people are. Circuses are loud, vulgar, and smell in the sun. By the time many people are fourteen or fifteen, they have been divested of their loves, their ancient and intuitive tastes, one by one, until when they reach maturity there is no fun left, no zest, no gusto, no flavor. Others have criticized, and they have criticized themselves, into embarrassment. When the circus pulls in at five of a dark cold summer morn, and the calliope sounds, they do not rise and run, they turn in their sleep, and life passes by.

I did rise and run. I learned that I was right and everyone else wrong when I was nine. Buck Rogers arrived on scene that year, and it was instant love. I collected the daily strips, and was madness maddened by them. Friends criticized. Friends made fun. I tore up the Buck Rogers strips. For a month I walked through my fourth-grade classes, stunned and empty. One day I burst into tears, wondering what devastation had happened to me. The answer was: Buck Rogers. He was gone, and life simply wasn't worth living. The next thought was: Those are not my friends, the ones who got me to tear the strips apart and so tear my own life down the middle; they are my enemies.

I went back to collecting Buck Rogers. My life has been happy ever since. For that was the beginning of my writing science fiction. Since then, I have never listened to anyone who criticized my taste in space travel, sideshows or gorillas. When this occurs, I pack up my dinosaurs and leave the room.

For, you see, it is all mulch. If I hadn't stuffed my eyes and stuffed my head with all of the above for a lifetime, when it came round to word-associating myself into story ideas, I would have brought up a ton of ciphers and a half-ton of zeros.

"The Veldt" is a prime example of what goes on in a headful of images, myths, toys. Back some thirty years ago I sat down to my typewriter one day and wrote these words: "The Playroom." Playroom where? The Past? No. The Present? Hardly. The Future? Yes! Well, then, what would a Playroom in some future year be like? I began typing, word-associating around the room. Such a Playroom must have television monitors lining each wall, and the ceiling. Walking into such an environment, a child could shout: River Nile! Sphinx! Pyramids! and they would appear, surrounding him, in full color, full sound, and, why not? Glorious warm scents and smells and odors, pick one, for the nose!

All this came to me in a few seconds of fast typing. I knew the room, now I must put characters in the room. I typed out a character named George, brought him into a future-time kitchen, where his wife turned and said:

"George, I wish you'd look at the Playroom. I think it's broken—"

George and his wife go down the hall. I follow them, typing madly, not knowing what will happen next. They open the door of the Playroom and step in.

Africa. Hot sun. Vultures. Dead meat. Lions.

Two hours later the lions leaped out of the walls of the Playroom and devoured George and his wife, while their TV-dominated children sat by and sipped tea.

End of word-association. End of story. The whole thing complete and almost ready to send out, an explosion of idea, in something like 120 minutes.

The lions in that room, where did they come from?

From the lions I found in the books in the town library when I was ten. From the lions I saw in the real circuses when I was five. From the lion that prowled in Lon Chaney's film *He Who Gets Slapped* in 1924!

In 1924! you say, with immense doubt. Yes, 1924. I didn't see the Chaney film again until a year ago. As soon as it flashed on the screen I knew that that was where my lions in "The Veldt" came from. They had been hiding out, waiting, given shelter by my intuitive self, all these years.

For I am that special freak, the man with the child inside who remembers all. I remember the day and the hour I was born. I remember being circumcised on the fourth day after my birth. I remember suckling at my mother's breast. Years later I asked my mother about the circumcision. I had information that couldn't have been told to me, there would be no reason to tell a child, especially in those still-Victorian times. Was I circumcised somewhere away from the lying-in hospital? I was. My father took me to the doctor's office. I remember the doctor. I remember the scalpel.

I wrote the story "The Small Assassin" twenty-six years later. It tells of a baby born with all its senses operative, filled with terror at being thrust out into a cold world, and taking revenge on its parents by crawling secretly about at night and at last destroying them.

When did it all really begin? The writing, that is. Everything came together in the summer and fall and early winter of 1932. By that time I was stuffed full of Buck Rogers, the novels of Edgar Rice Burroughs, and the night-time radio serial "Chandu the Magician." Chandu said magic and the psychic summons and the Far East and strange places which made me sit down every night and from memory write out the scripts of each show.

But the whole conglomeration of magic and myths and falling downstairs with brontosaurs only to arise with La of Opar, was shaken into a pattern by one man, Mr. Electrico.

He arrived with a seedy two-bit carnival, The Dill Brothers Combined Shows, during Labor Day weekend of 1932, when I was twelve. Every night for three nights, Mr. Electrico sat in his electric chair, being fired with ten billion volts of pure blue sizzling power. Reaching out into the audience, his eyes flaming, his white hair standing on end, sparks leaping between his smiling teeth, he brushed an Excalibur sword over the heads of the children, knighting them with fire. When he came to me, he tapped me on both shoulders and then the tip of my nose. The lightning jumped into me. Mr. Electrico cried: *"Live forever!"*

I decided that was the greatest idea I had ever heard. I went to see Mr. Electrico the next day, with the excuse that a nickel magic trick I had purchased from him wasn't in working order. He fixed it, and toured me around the tents, shouting at each, "Clean up your language," before we entered to meet the dwarfs, acrobats, fat women, and Illustrated Men waiting there.

We walked down to sit by Lake Michigan where Mr. Electrico spoke his small philosophies and I talked my big ones. Why he put up with me, I'll never know. But he listened, or it seemed he listened, maybe because he was far from home, maybe because he had a son somewhere in the world, or had no son at all and wanted one. Anyway he was a defrocked Presbyterian minister, he said, and lived down in Cairo, Illinois, and I could write him there, any time I wished.

Finally he gave me some special news.

"We've met before," he said. "You were my best friend in France in 1918, and you died in my arms in the battle of the Ardennes forest that year. And here your are, born again, in a new body, with a new name. Welcome back!"

I staggered away from that encounter with Mr. Electrico wonderfully uplifted by two gifts: the gift of having lived once before (and being told about it) . . . and the gift of trying somehow to live forever.

A few weeks later I started writing my first short stories about the planet Mars. From that time to this, I have never stopped. God bless Mr. Electrico, the catalyst, wherever he is.

If I consider every aspect of all the above, my beginnings almost inevitably had to be in the attic. From the time I was twelve until I was twenty-two or -three, I wrote stories long after midnight—unconventional stories of ghosts and haunts and things in jars that I had seen in sour armpit carnivals, of friends lost to the tides in lakes, and of consorts of three in the morning, those souls who had to fly in the dark in order not to be shot in the sun.

It took me many years to write myself down out of the attic, where I had to make do with my own eventual mortality (a teenagers' preoccupation), make it to the living room, then out to the lawn and sunlight where the dandelions had come up, ready for wine.

Getting out on the front lawn with my Fourth of July relatives gave me not only my Green Town, Illinois, stories, it also shoved me off toward Mars, following Edgar Rice Burroughs's and John Carter's advice, taking my childhood luggage, my uncles, aunts, my mom, dad, and brother with me. When I arrived on Mars I found them, in fact, waiting for me, or Martians who looked like them, pretending me into a grave. The Green Town stories that found their way into an accidental novel titled *Dandelion Wine* and the Red Planet stories that blundered into another accidental novel called *The Martian Chronicles* were written, alternately, during the same years that I ran to the rainbarrel outside my grandparents' house to dip out all the memories, the myths, the word-associations of other years.

Along the way, I also re-created my relatives as vampires who inhabited a town similar to the one in *Dandelion Wine*, dark first cousin to the town on Mars where the Third Expedition expired. So, I had my life three ways, as town explorer, space traveler, and wanderer with Count Dracula's American cousins.

I realize I haven't talked half enough, as yet, about one variety of creature you will find stalking this collection, rising here in nightmares to founder there in loneliness and despair: dinosaurs. From the time I was seventeen until I was thirty-two, I wrote some half-dozen dinosaur stories.

One night when my wife and I were walking along the beach in Venice, California, where we lived in a thirty-dollar-a-month newlyweds' apartment, we came upon the bones of the Venice Pier and the struts, tracks, and ties of the ancient roller-coaster collapsed on the sand and being eaten by the sea.

"What's that dinosaur doing lying here on the beach?" I said.

My wife, very wisely, had no answer.

The answer came the next night when, summoned from sleep by a voice calling, I rose up, listened, and heard the lonely voice of the Santa Monica bay fog horn blowing over and over and over again.

Of course! I thought. The dinosaur heard that lighthouse fog horn blowing, thought it was another dinosaur arisen from the deep past, came swimming in for a loving confrontation, discovered it was only a fog horn, and died of a broken heart there on the shore.

I leaped from bed, wrote the story, and sent it to the *Saturday Evening Post* that week, where it appeared soon after under the title "The Beast from 20,000 Fathoms." That story, titled "The Fog Horn" in this collection, became a film two years later.

The story was read by John Huston in 1953, who promptly called to ask if I would like to write the screenplay for his film *Moby Dick*. I accepted, and moved from one beast to the next.

Because of *Moby Dick*, I reexamined the life of Melville and Jules Verne, compared their mad captains in an essay written to reintroduce a new translation of *20,000 Leagues Beneath the Sea*, which, read by the 1964 New York World's Fair people, put me in charge of conceptualizing the entire upper floor of the United States Pavilion.

Because of the Pavilion, the Disney organization hired me to help plan the dreams that went into Spaceship Earth, part of Epcot Center, a permanent world's fair. In that one building, I have crammed a history of mankind, coming and going back and forth in time, then plunging into our wild future in space.

Including dinosaurs.

All of my activities, all of my growing, all of my new jobs and new loves, caused and created by that original primitive love of the beasts I saw when I was five and dearly cherished when I was twenty and twenty-nine and thirty.

Look around among my stories and you will probably find only one or two that actually happened to me. I have resisted, most of my life, being given assignments to go somewhere and "sponge up" the local color, the natives, the look and feel of the land. I learned long ago that I am not seeing directly, that my subconscious is doing most of the "sponging" and it will be years before any usable impressions surface.

As a young man I lived in a tenement in the Chicano section of Los Angeles. Most of my Latino stories were written years after I had moved from the tenement, with one terrifying, on-the-spot, exception. In late 1945, with World War II freshly over, a friend of mine asked me to accompany him to Mexico City in an old beat-up Ford V-8. I reminded him of the vow of poverty that circumstances had forced on me. He rebutted by calling me a coward, wondering why I didn't rev up my courage and send out three or four stories which I had hidden away. Reason for the hiding: the stories had been rejected once or twice by various magazines. Pummeled by my friend, I dusted the stories off and mailed them out, under the pseudonym William Elliott. Why the pseudonym? Because I feared that some Manhattan editors might have seen the name Bradbury on the covers of *Weird Tales* and would be prejudiced against this "pulp" writer.

I mailed off three short stories to three different magazines, in the second week of August 1945. On August 20, I sold one story to *Charm*, on August 21, I sold a story to *Mademoiselle*, and on August 22, my twenty-fifth birthday, I sold a story to *Collier's*. The total monies amounted to $1,000, which would be like having $10,000 arrive in the mail today.

I was rich. Or so close to it I was dumbfounded. It was a turning point in my life, of course, and I hastened to write to the editors of those three magazines confessing my true name.

All three stories were listed in *The Best American Short Stories of 1946* by Martha Foley, and one of them was published in Herschel Brickell's O. Henry Memorial Award *Prize Stories* the following year.

That money took me to Mexico, to Guanajuato, and the mummies in the catacombs. The experience so wounded and terrified me, I could hardly wait to flee Mexico. I had nightmares about dying and having to remain in the halls of the dead with those propped and wired bodies. In order to purge my terror, instantly, I wrote "The Next in Line." One of the few times that an experience yielded results almost on the spot.

Enough of Mexico. What about Ireland?

There is every kind of Irish story among my work because after living in Dublin for six months I saw that most of the Irish I met had a variety of ways of making do with that dreadful beast Reality. You can run into it head-on, which is a dire business, or you can skirt around it, give it a poke, dance for it, make up a song, write you a tale, prolong the gab, fill up the flask. Each partakes of Irish cliché, but each, in the foul weather and the foundering politics, is true.

I got to know every beggar in the streets of Dublin, the ones near O'Connell's bridge with maniac pianolas grinding more coffee than tunes and the ones who loaned out a single baby among a whole tribe of rainsoaked mendicants, so you saw the babe one hour at the top of Grafton Street and the next by the Royal Hibernian Hotel, and at midnight down by the river, but I never thought I would write of them. Then, the need to howl and give an angry weep made me rear up one night and write "McGillahee's Brat" out of terrible suspicions and the begging of a rainwalking ghost that had to be laid. I visited some of the old burnt-out estates of the great Irish landowners, and heard tales of one "burning" that had not quite come off, and so wrote "The Terrible Conflagration up at the Place."

"The Anthem Sprinters," another Irish encounter, wrote itself down years later when, one rainy night, I recalled the countless times my wife and I had sprinted out of Dublin cinemas, dashing for the exit, knocking children and old folks to left and right, in order to make it to the exit before the National Anthem was played.

But how did I begin? Starting in Mr. Electrico's year, I wrote a thousand words a day. For ten years I wrote at least one short story a week, somehow guessing that a day would finally come when I truly got out of the way and let it happen.

The day came in 1942 when I wrote "The Lake." Ten years of doing everything wrong suddenly became the right idea, the right scene, the right characters, the right day, the right creative time. I wrote the story sitting outside, with my typewriter, on the lawn. At the end of an hour the story was finished, the hair on the back of my neck was standing up, and I was in tears. I knew I had written the first really good story of my life.

All during my early twenties I had the following

schedule. On Monday morning I wrote the first draft of a new story. On Tuesday I did a second draft. On Wednesday a third. On Thursday a fourth. On Friday a fifth. And on Saturday at noon I mailed out the sixth and final draft to New York. Sunday? I thought about all the wild ideas scrambling for my attention, waiting under the attic lid, confident at last that, because of "The Lake," I would soon let them out.

If this all sounds mechanical, it wasn't. My ideas drove me to it, you see. The more I did, the more I wanted to do. You grow ravenous. You run fevers. You know exhilarations. You can't sleep at night, because your beast-creature ideas want out and turn you in your bed. It is a grand way to live.

There was another reason to write so much: I was being paid twenty to forty dollars a story, by the pulp magazines. High on the hog was hardly my way of life. I had to sell at least one story, or better two, each month in order to survive my hot-dog, hamburger, trolley-car-fare life.

In 1944 I sold some forty stories, but my total income for the year was only $800.

It suddenly strikes me that there is much to comment on in my collected stories. "The Black Ferris" is of interest here because early one autumn twenty-three years ago it changed itself from a short short story into a screenplay and then into a novel, *Something Wicked This Way Comes*.

"The Day It Rained Forever" was another word-association I handed myself one afternoon, thinking about hot suns, deserts, and harps that could change the weather.

"The Leave-Taking" is the true story of my great-grandmother who nailed shingles on rooftops well into her seventies, then took herself up to bed when I was three and said farewell to everyone and went to sleep.

"Calling Mexico" spring into being because I visited a friend of mine one afternoon in the summer of 1946 and, as I entered the room, he handed me the telephone and said, "Listen." I listened and heard the sounds of Mexico City coming from two thousand miles away. I went home and wrote about my telephone experience to a friend in Paris. Halfway through my letter, the letter turned into the story, which went off in the mail that day.

"The Picasso Summer" was the result of my walking on the shoreline with friends and my wife one late afternoon. I picked up a Popsicle stick, drew pictures in the sand and said: "Wouldn't it be awful, if you'd wanted to own a Picasso all your life, and suddenly bumped into him here, drawing mythological beasts in the sand . . . your very own Picasso 'etching' right in front of you. . . ."

I finished the story, about Picasso on the beach, at two in the morning.

Hemingway. "The Parrot Who Met Papa." One

night in 1952 I drove across Los Angeles with friends to invade the printing plant where *Life* was publishing their issue with Hemingway's *Old Man and the Sea* in it. We grabbed copies, hot off the press, sat in the nearest bar, and talked about Papa, Finca Vigía, Cuba, and, somehow, a parrot who had lived in that bar and talked to Hemingway every night. I went home, made a notation about the parrot, and put it away for sixteen years. Prowling my file folders in 1968 I came upon just the note for a title: "The Parrot Who Met Papa."

My God, I thought, Papa's been dead eight years. If that parrot is still around, remembers Hemingway, can speak with his voice, he's worth millions. And what if someone kidnapped the parrot, held it for ransom?

"The Haunting of the New" happened because John Godley, Lord Kilbracken, wrote me from Ireland describing his visit to a house that had burned and been replaced, stone by stone, brick by brick, in imitation of the original. Within half a day of reading Kilbracken's postcard, I had first-drafted the tale.

Enough now. There you have it. There are one hundred stories from almost forty years of my life contained in my collected stories. They contain half the damning truths I suspected at midnight, and half of the saying truths I re-found next noon. If anything is taught here, it is simply the charting of the life of someone who started out to somewhere—and went. I have not so much thought my way through life as done things and found what it was and who I was after the doing. Each tale was a way of finding selves. Each self found each day slightly different from the one found twenty-four hours earlier.

It all started that autumn day in 1932 when Mr. Electrico gave me the two gifts. I don't know if I believe in previous lives, I'm not sure I can live forever. But that young boy believed in both and I have let him have his head. He has written my stories and books for me. He runs the Ouija Board and says Aye or Nay to submerged truths or half-truths. He is the skin through which, by osmosis, all the stuffs pass and put themselves on paper. I have trusted his passions, his fears, and his joys. He has, as a result, rarely failed me. When it is a long damp November in my soul, and I think too much and perceive too little, I know it is high time to get back to that boy with the tennis shoes, the high fevers, the multitudinous joys, and the terrible nightmares. I'm not sure where he leaves off and I start. But I'm proud of the tandem team. What else can I do but wish him well, and at the same time acknowledge and wish two other people well? In the same month that I married my wife Marguerite, I became affiliated with my literary representative and closest friend, Don Congdon. Maggie typed and criticized my stories, Don criticized and sold the results. With the two of them as teammates these past thirty-three years, how could I have failed? We are the Connemara Lightfoots, the Queen's Own Evaders. And we're still sprinting for that exit.

1980

INVESTING DIMES:

FAHRENHEIT 451

I didn't know it, but I was literally writing a dime novel. In the spring of 1950 it cost me nine dollars and eighty cents to write and finish the first draft of *The Fire Man*, which later became *Fahrenheit 451*.

In all the years from 1941 to that time, I had done most of my typing in the family garages, either in Venice, California (where we lived because we were poor, not because it was the "in" place to be), or behind the tract house where my wife, Marguerite, and I raised our family. I was driven out of my garage by my loving children, who insisted on coming around to the rear window and singing and tapping on the panes. Father had to choose between finishing a story or playing with the girls. I chose to play, of course, which endangered the family income. An office had to be found. We couldn't afford one.

Finally, I located just the place, the typing room in the basement of the library at the University of California at Los Angeles. There, in neat rows, were a score or more of old Remington or Underwood typewriters which rented out at a dime a half hour. You thrust your dime in, the clock ticked madly, and you typed wildly, to finish before the half hour ran out. Thus I was twice driven; by children to leave home, and by a typewriter timing device to be a maniac at the keys. Time was indeed money. I finished the first draft in roughly nine days. At 25,000 words, it was half the novel it eventually would become.

Between investing dimes and going insane when the typewriter jammed (for there went your precious time!) and whipping pages in and out of the device, I wandered upstairs. There I strolled, lost in love, down the corridors, and through the stacks, touching books, pulling volumes out, turning pages, thrusting volumes back, drowning in all the good stuffs that are the essence of libraries. What a place, don't you agree, to write a novel about burning books in the Future!

So much for pasts. What about *Fahrenheit 451* in this day and age? Have I changed my mind about much that it said to me, when I was a younger writer? Only if by change you mean has my love of libraries widened and deepened, to which the answer is a yes that ricochets off the stacks and dusts talcum off the librarian's cheek. Since writing this book, I have spun more stories, novels, essays, and poems about writers than any other writer in history that I can think of. I have written poems about Melville, Melville and Emily Dickinson, Emily Dickinson and Charles Dickens, Hawthorne, Poe, Edgar Rice Burroughs, and along the way I compared Jules Verne and his Mad Captain to Melville and his equally obsessed mariner. I have scribbled poems about librarians, taken night trains with my favorite authors across the continental wilderness, staying up all night gabbling and drinking, drinking and chatting. I warned Melville, in one poem, to stay away from land (it never was his stuff!) and turned Bernard Shaw into a robot, so as to conveniently stow him aboard a rocket and wake him on the long journey to Alpha Centauri to hear his Prefaces piped off his tongue and into my delighted ear. I have written a Time Machine story in which I hum back to sit at the deathbeds of Wilde, Melville, and Poe to tell of my love and warm their bones in their last hours. . . . But, enough. As you can see, I am madness—maddened when it comes to books, writers, and the great granary silos where their wits are stored.

Recently, with the Studio Theatre Playhouse in Los Angeles at hand, I called all my characters from F. 451 out of the shadows. What's new, I said to Montag, Clarisse, Faber, Beatty, since last we met in 1953?

I asked. *They* answered.

They wrote new scenes, revealed odd parts of their as yet undiscovered souls and dreams. The result was a two-act drama, staged with good results, and in the main, fine reviews.

Beatty came farthest out of the wings in answer to

my question: How did it start? Why did you make the decision to become Fire Chief, a burner of books? Beatty's surprising answer came in a scene where he takes our hero Guy Montag home to his apartment. Entering, Montag is stunned to discover the thousands upon thousands of books lining the walls of the Fire Chief's hidden library! Montag turns and cries out to his superior:

"But you're the Chief Burner! You can't have books on your premises!"

To which the Chief, with a dry light smile, replies:

"It's not *owning* books that's a crime, Montag, it's *reading* them! Yes, that's right. I own books, but don't *read* them!"

Montag, in shock, awaits Beatty's explanation.

"Don't you see the beauty, Montag? I never read them. Not one book, not one chapter, not one page, not one paragraph. I *do* play with ironies, don't I? To have thousands of books and never crack one, to turn your back on the lot and say: No. It's like having a house full of beautiful women and, smiling, not touching . . . one. So, you see, I'm not a criminal at all. If you ever catch me *reading* one, yes, then turn me in! But this place is as pure as a twelve-year-old virgin girl's cream-white summer night bedroom. These books die on the shelves. Why? Because I say so. I do not give them sustenance, no hope with hand or eye or tongue. They are no better than dust."

Montag protests. "I don't see how you can't be—"

"Tempted?" cries the Fire Chief. "Oh, *that* was long ago. The apple is eaten and gone. The snake has returned to its tree. The garden has grown to weed and rust."

"Once—" Montag hesitates, then continues, "Once you must have loved books very much."

"Touché!" the Fire Chief responds. "Below the belt. On the chin. Through the heart. Ripping the gut. Oh, look at me, Montag. The man who loved books, no, the boy who was wild for them, insane for them, who climbed the stacks like a chimpanzee gone mad for them.

"I ate them like salad, books were my sandwich for lunch, my tiffin and dinner and midnight munch. I tore out the pages, ate them with salt, doused them with relish, gnawed on the bindings, turned the chapters with my tongue! Books by the dozen, the score and the billion. I carried so many home I was hunchbacked for years. Philosophy, art history, politics, social science, the poem, the essay, the grandiose play, you name 'em. I ate 'em. And then . . . and then . . ." The Fire Chief's voice fades.

Montag prompts: "And then?"

"Why, life happened to me." The Fire Chief shuts his eyes to remember. "Life. The usual. The same. The love that wasn't quite right, the dream that went sour, the sex that fell apart, the deaths that came swiftly to friends not deserving, the murder of some-one or another, the insanity of someone close, the slow death of a mother, the abrupt suicide of a father—a stampede of elephants, an onslaught of disease. And nowhere, nowhere the right book for the right time to stuff in the crumbling wall of the breaking dam to hold back the deluge, give or take a metaphor, lose or find a simile. And by the far edge of thirty, and the near rim of thirty-one, I picked myself up, every bone broken, every centimeter of flesh abraded, bruised, or scarred. I looked in the mirror and found an old man lost behind the frightened face of a young man, saw a hatred there for everything and anything, you name it, I'd damn it, and opened the pages of my fine library books and found what, what, what!?"

Montag guesses. "The pages were empty?"

"Bull's eye! Blank! Oh, the words were there, allright, but they ran over my eyes like hot oil, signifying nothing. Offering no help, no solace, no peace, no harbor, no true love, no bed, no light."

Montag thinks back: "Thirty years ago . . . the final library burnings. . . ."

"On target." Beatty nods. "And having no job, and being a failed Romantic, or whatever in hell, I put in for Fireman First Class. First up the steps, first into the library, first in the burning furnace heart of his ever-blazing countrymen, douse me with kerosene, hand me my torch!

"End of lecture. There you go, Montag. Out the door!"

Montag leaves, with more curiosity than ever about books, well on his way to becoming an outcast, soon to be pursued and almost destroyed by the Mechanical Hound, my robot clone of A. Conan Doyle's great Baskerville beast.

In my play, old man Faber, the teacher-not-quite-in-residence, speaking to Montag through the long night (via the seashell tamp-in ear radio) is victimized by the Fire Chief. How? Beatty suspects Montag is being instructed by such a secret device, knocks it out of his ear, and shouts at the far-removed teacher:

"We're coming to get you! We're at the door! We're up the stairs! Gotcha!"

Which so terrifies Faber, his heart destroys him.

All good stuff. Tempting, this late in time. I've had to fight not to stuff it into the novel.

Finally, many readers have written protesting Clarisse's disappearance, wondering what happened to her. François Truffaut felt the same curiosity, and in his film version of my novel, rescued Clarisse from oblivion and located her with the Book People wandering in the forest, reciting their litany of books to themselves. I felt the same need to save her, for after all, she, verging on silly star-struck chatter, was in many ways responsible for Montag's beginning to wonder about books and what was in them. In my play, therefore, Clarisse emerges to welcome Montag, and give a somewhat happier ending to what was, in essence, pretty grim stuff.

The novel, however, remains true to its former self. I don't believe in tampering with any young writer's material, especially when that young writer was once myself. Montag, Beatty, Mildred, Faber, Clarisse, all stand, move, enter and exit as they did thirty-two years ago when I first wrote them down, at a dime a half hour, in the basement of the UCLA library. I have changed not one thought or word.

A last discovery. I write all of my novels and stories, as you have seen, in a great surge of delightful passion. Only recently, glancing at the novel, I realized that Montag is named after a paper manufacturing company. And Faber, of course, is a maker of pencils! What a sly thing my subconscious was, to name them thus.

And not tell *me*!

1982

JUST THIS SIDE OF

BYZANTIUM:

DANDELION WINE

Dandelion Wine like most of my books and stories, was a surprise. I began to learn the nature of such surprises, thank God, when I was fairly young as a writer. Before that, like every beginner, I thought you could beat, pummel, and thrash an idea into existence. Under such treatment, of course, any decent idea folds up its paws, turns on its back, fixes its eyes on eternity, and dies.

It was with great relief, then, that in my early twenties I floundered into a word-association process in which I simply got out of bed each morning, walked to my desk, and put down any word or series of words that happened along in my head.

I would then take arms against the word, or for it, and bring on an assortment of characters to weigh the word and show me its meaning in my own life. An hour or two hours later, to my amazement, a new story would be finished and done. The surprise was total and lovely. I soon found that I would have to work this way for the rest of my life.

First I rummaged my mind for words that could describe my personal nightmares, fears of night and time from my childhood, and shaped stories from these.

Then I took a long look at the green apple trees and the old house I was born in and the house next door where lived my grandparents, and all the lawns of the summers I grew up in, and I began to try words for all that.

What you have in *Dandelion Wine* then is a gathering of dandelions from all those years. The wine metaphor which appears again and again in these pages is wonderfully apt. I was gathering images all of my life, storing them away, and forgetting them. Somehow I had to send myself back, with words as catalysts, to open the memories out and see what they had to offer.

So from the age of twenty-four to thirty-six hardly a day passed when I didn't stroll myself across a recollection of my grandparents' northern Illinois grass, hoping to come across some old half-burnt firecracker, a rusted toy, or a fragment of letter written to myself in some young year hoping to contact the older person I became to remind him of his past, his life, his people, his joys, and his drenching sorrows.

It became a game that I took to with immense gusto: to see how much I could remember about dandelions themselves, or picking wild grapes with my father and brother, rediscovering the mosquito-breeding ground rain barrel by the side bay window, or searching out the smell of the gold-fuzzed bees that hung around our back porch grape arbor. Bees do have a smell, you know, and if they don't they should, for their feet are dusted with spices from a million flowers.

And then I wanted to call back what the ravine was like, especially on those nights when walking home late across town, after seeing Lon Chaney's delicious fright *The Phantom of the Opera*, my brother Skip would run ahead and hide under the ravine-creek bridge like the Lonely One and leap out and grab me, shrieking, so I ran, fell, and ran again, gibbering all the way home. That was great stuff.

Along the way, I came upon and collided, through word-association, with old and true friendships. I borrowed my friend John Huff from my childhood in Arizona and shipped him East to Green Town so that I could say goodbye to him properly.

Along the way, I sat me down to breakfasts, lunches, and dinners with the long dead and much loved. For I was a boy who did indeed love his parents and grandparents and his brother, even when that brother "ditched" him.

Along the way, I found myself in the basement working the wine-press for my father, or on the front porch Independence night helping my Uncle Bion load and fire his homemade brass cannon.

Thus I fell into surprise. No one told me to surprise myself, I might add. I came on the old and best ways of writing through ignorance and experiment and was startled when truths leaped out of bushes like quail before gunshot. I blundered into creativity as blindly as any child learning to walk and see. I learned to let my senses and my Past tell me all that was somehow true.

So, I turned myself into a boy running to bring a dipper of clear rainwater out of that barrel by the side of the house. And, of course, the more water you dip out the more flows in. The flow has never ceased. Once I learned to keep going back and back again to those times, I had plenty of memories and sense impressions to play with, not work with, no, play with. *Dandelion Wine* is nothing if it is not the boy-hid-in-the-man playing in the fields of the Lord on the green grass of other Augusts in the midst of starting to grow up, grow old, and sense darkness waiting under the trees to seed the blood.

I was amused and somewhat astonished at a critic a few years back who wrote an article analyzing *Dandelion Wine* plus the more realistic works of Sinclair Lewis, wondering how I could have been born and raised in Waukegan, which I renamed Green Town for my novel, and not noticed how ugly the harbor was and how depressing the coal docks and railyards down below the town.

But, of course, I had noticed them and, genetic enchanter that I was, was fascinated by their beauty. Trains and boxcars and the smell of coal and fire are not ugly to children. Ugliness is a concept that we happen on later and become self-conscious about. Counting boxcars is a prime activity of boys. Their elders fret and fume and jeer at the train that holds them up, but boys happily count and cry the names of the cars as they pass from far places.

And again, that supposedly ugly railyard was where carnivals and circuses arrived with elephants who washed the brick pavements with mighty steaming acid waters at five in the dark morning.

As for the coal from the docks, I went down in my basement every autumn to await the arrival of the truck and its metal chute, which clanged down and released a ton of beauteous meteors that fell out of far space into my cellar and threatened to bury me beneath dark treasures.

In other words, if your boy is a poet, horse manure can only mean flowers to him; which is, of course, what horse manure has always been about.

Perhaps a new poem of mine will explain more than this introduction about the germination of all the summers of my life into one book.

Here's the start of the poem:

> Byzantium, I come not from,
> But from another time and place
> Whose race was simple, tried and true;
> As boy
> I dropped me forth in Illinois.

A name with neither love nor grace
Was Waukegan, there I came from
And not, good friends, Byzantium.

The poem continues, describing my lifelong relationship to my birthplace:

And yet in looking back I see
From topmost part of farthest tree
A land as bright, beloved and
blue
As any Yeats found to be true.

Waukegan, visited by me often since, is neither homelier nor more beautiful than any other small midwestern town. Much of it is green. The trees *do* touch in the middle of streets. The street in front of my old home is still paved with red bricks. In what way then was the town special? Why, I was born there. It was my life. I had to write of it as I saw fit:

So we grew up with mythic dead
To spoon upon midwestern bread
And spread old gods' bright marmalade
To slake in peanut-butter shade,
Pretending there beneath our sky
That it was Aphrodite's thigh . . .
While by the porch-rail calm and bold

His words pure wisdom, stare pure gold
My grandfather, a myth indeed,
Did all of Plato supersede
While Grandmama in rockingchair
Sewed up the raveled sleeve of care
Crocheted cool snowflakes rare and bright
To winter us on summer night.
And uncles, gathered with their smokes
Emitted wisdoms masked as jokes,
And aunts as wise as Delphic maids
Dispensed prophetic lemonades
To boys knelt there as acolytes
To Grecian porch on summer nights;
Then went to bed, there to repent
The evils of the innocent;
The gnat-sins sizzling in their ears
Said, through the nights and through the years
Not Illinois nor Waukegan
But blither sky and blither sun.
Though mediocre all our Fates
And Mayor not as bright as Yeats
Yet still we knew ourselves. The sum?
Byzantium.
Byzantium.

Waukegan/Green Town/Byzantium.
Green Town *did* exist, then?
Yes, and again, yes.

Was there a real boy named John Huff?

There was. And that was truly his name. But he didn't go away from me, I went away from him. But, happy ending, he is still alive, forty-two years later, and remembers our love.

Was there a Lonely One?

There was, and that was *his* name. And he moved around at night in my home town when I was six years old and he frightened everyone and was never captured.

Most importantly, did the big house itself, with Grandpa and Grandma and the boarders and uncles and aunts in it exist? I have already answered that.

Is the ravine real and deep and dark at night? It was, it is. I took my daughters there a few years back, fearful that the ravine might have gone shallow with time. I am relieved and happy to report that the ravine is deeper, darker, and more mysterious than ever. I would not, even now, go home through there after seeing *The Phantom of the Opera*.

So there you have it. Waukegan was Green Town was Byzantium, with all the happiness that that means, with all the sadness that these names imply. The people there were gods and midgets and knew themselves mortal and so the midgets walked tall so as not to embarrass the gods and the gods crouched so as to make the small ones feel at home. And, after all, isn't that what life is all about, the ability to go around back and come up inside other people's heads to look out at the damned fool miracle and say: oh, so that's how you see it!? Well, now, I must remember that.

Here is my celebration, then, of death as well as life, dark as well as light, old as well as young, smart and dumb combined, sheer joy as well as complete terror written by a boy who once hung upside down in trees, dressed in his bat costume with candy fangs in his mouth, who finally fell out of the trees when he was twelve and went and found a toy-dial typewriter and wrote his first "novel."

A final memory.

Fire balloons.

You rarely see them these days, though in some countries, I hear, they are still made and filled with warm breath from a small straw fire hung beneath.

But in 1925 Illinois, we still had them, and one of the last memories I have of my grandfather is the last hour of a Fourth of July night forty-eight years ago when Grandpa and I walked out on the lawn and lit a small fire and filled the pear-shaped red-white-and-blue-striped paper balloon with hot air, and held the flickering bright-angel presence in our hands a final moment in front of a porch lined with uncles and aunts and cousins and mothers and fathers, and then, very softly, let the thing that was life and light and mystery go out of our fingers up on the summer air and away over the beginning-to-sleep houses, among the stars, as fragile, as wondrous, as vulnerable, as lovely as life itself.

I see my grandfather there looking up at that strange drifting light, thinking his own still thoughts. I see me, my eyes filled with tears, because it was all over, the night was done, I knew there would never be another night like this.

No one said anything. We all just looked up at the sky and we breathed out and in and we all thought the same things, but nobody said. Someone finally had to say, though, didn't they? And that one is me.

The wine still waits in the cellars below.

My beloved family still sits on the porch in the dark.

The fire balloon still drifts and burns in the night sky of an as yet unburied summer.

Why and how?

Because I say it is so.

1974

ON THE SHOULDERS

OF GIANTS

DUSK IN THE ROBOT MUSEUMS: THE REBIRTH OF IMAGINATION

～～～ For some ten years now, I have been writing a long narrative poem about a small boy in the near future who runs into an audio-animatronic museum, veers away from the right portico marked *Rome*, passes a door marked *Alexandria*, and enters across a sill where a sign lettered *Greece* points in across a meadow.

The boy runs over the artificial grass and comes upon Plato, Socrates and perhaps Euripides seated at high noon under an olive tree sipping wine and eating bread and honey and speaking truths.

The boy hesitates and then addresses Plato:

"How goes it with the Republic?"

"Sit down, boy," says Plato, "and I'll tell you."

The boy sits. Plato tells. Socrates steps in from time to time. Euripides does a scene from one of his plays.

Along the way, the boy might well ask a question which hovered in all of our minds the past few decades:

"How come the United States, *the* country of Ideas on the March, for so long neglected fantasy and science fiction? Why is it that only during the past thirty years attention is being paid?"

Another question from the boy might well be:

"Who is responsible for the change?

"Who has taught the teachers and the librarians to pull up their socks, sit straight, and take notice?

"Simultaneously, which group in our country has backed off from abstraction and moved art back in the direction of pure illustration?"

Since I am neither dead nor a robot, and Plato-as-audio-animatronic lecturer might not be programmed to respond, let me answer as best I can.

The answer is: the students. The young people. The children.

They have led the revolution in reading and painting.

For the first time in the history of art and teaching, the children have become the teachers. Before our time, knowledge came down from the top of the pyramid to the broad base where the students survived as best they could. The gods spoke and the children listened.

But, lo! gravity reverses itself. The massive pyramid turns like a melting iceberg, until the boys and girls are on top. The base of the pyramid now teaches.

How did it happen? After all, back in the twenties and thirties, there were no science-fiction books in the curricula of schools anywhere. There were few in the libraries. Only once or twice a year did a responsible publisher dare to publish one or two books which could be designated as speculative fiction.

If you went into the average library as you motored across America in 1932, 1945, or 1953 you would have found:

No Edgar Rice Burroughs.

No L. Frank Baum and no *Oz*.

In 1958 or 1962 you would have found no Asimov, no Heinlein, no Van Vogt, and, er, no Bradbury.

Here and there, perhaps one book or two by the above. For the rest: a desert.

What were the reasons for this?

Among librarians and teachers there was then, and there still somewhat dimly persists, an idea, a notion, a concept that only Fact should be eaten with your Wheaties. Fantasy? That's for the Fire Birds. Fantasy, even when it takes science-fictional forms, which it often does, is dangerous. It is escapist. It is daydreaming. It has nothing to do with the world and the world's problems.

So said the snobs who did not know themselves as snobs.

So the shelves lay empty, the books untouched in publishers' bins, the subject untaught.

Comes the Evolution. The survival of that species called Child. The children, dying of starvation, hungry for ideas which lay all about in this fabulous land, locked into machines and architecture, struck out on their own. What did they do?

They walked into classrooms in Waukesha and Peoria and Neepawa and Cheyenne and Moose Jaw and Redwood City and placed a gentle bomb on teacher's desk. Instead of an apple it was Asimov.

"What's that?" the teacher asked, suspiciously.

"Try it. It's good for you," said the students.

"No thanks."

"Try it," said the students. "Read the first page. If you don't like it, stop." And the clever students turned and went away.

The teachers (and the librarians, later) put off reading, kept the book around the house for a few weeks and then, late one night, tried the first paragraph.

And the bomb exploded.

They not only read the first but the second paragraph, the second and third pages, the fourth and fifth chapters.

"My God!" they cried, almost in unison, "these damned books are *about* something!"

"Good Lord!" they cried, reading a second book, "there are Ideas here!"

"Holy Smoke!" they babbled, on their way through Clarke, heading into Heinlein, emerging from Sturgeon, "these books are—ugly word—relevant!"

"Yes!" shouted the chorus of kids starving in the yard. "Oh, my, yes!"

And the teachers began to teach, and discovered an amazing thing:

Students who had never wanted to read before suddenly were galvanized, pulled up *their* socks, and began to read and quote Ursula Le Guin. Kids who had never read so much as one pirate's obituary in their lives, were suddenly turning pages with their tongues, ravening for more.

Librarians were stunned to find that science-fiction books were not only being borrowed in the tens of thousands, but stolen and never returned!

"Where have we been?" the librarians and the teachers asked each other, as the Prince kissed them awake. "What's *in* these books that makes them as irresistible as Cracker Jack?"

The History of Ideas.

The children wouldn't have said it in so many words. They only sensed it and read it and loved it. The kids sensed, if they could not speak it, that the first science-fiction writers were cavemen who were trying to figure out the first sciences—which were what? How to capture fire. What to do about that lout of a mammoth hanging around outside the cave. How to play dentist to the sabre-tooth tiger and turn him into a house-cat.

Pondering those problems and possible sciences, the first cavemen and women drew science-fiction dreams on the cave walls. Scribbles in soot blueprinting possible strategies. Illustrations of mammoths, tigers, fires: how to solve? How to turn science-fiction (problem solving) into science-fact (problem solved).

Some few brave ones ran out of the cave to be stomped by the mammoth, toothed by the tiger, scorched by the bestial fire that lived on trees and devoured wood. Some few finally returned to draw on the walls the triumph of the mammoth knocked like a hairy cathedral to earth, the tiger toothless, and the fire tamed and brought within the cave to light their nightmares and warm their souls.

The children sensed, if they could not speak, that the entire history of mankind is problem solving, or science fiction swallowing ideas, digesting them, and excreting formulas for survival. You can't have one without the other. No fantasy, no reality. No studies concerning loss, no gain. No imagination, no will. No impossible dreams: No possible solutions.

The children sensed, if they could not say, that fantasy, and its robot child science fiction, is not escape at all. But a circling round of reality to enchant it and make it behave. What is an airplane, after all, but a circling of reality, an approach to gravity which says: Look, with my magic machine, I defy you. Gravity be gone. Distance, stand aside. Time, stand still, or reverse, as I finally outrace the sun around the world in, by God! look! plane/jet/rocket—80 minutes!

The children guessed, if they did not whisper it,

that all science fiction is an attempt to solve problems by pretending to look the other way.

In another place I have described this literary process as Perseus confronted by Medusa. Gazing at Medusa's image in his bronze shield, pretending to look one way, Perseus reaches back over his shoulder and severs Medusa's head. So science fiction pretends at futures in order to cure sick dogs lying in today's road. Indirection is everything. Metaphor is the medicine.

Children love cataphracts, though do not name them thusly. A cataphract is only a special Persian on a specially bred horse, the combination of which threw back the Roman legions some long while ago. Problem solving. Problem: massive Roman armies on foot. Science fiction dreams: cataphract/man-on-horseback. Romans dispersed. Problem solved. Science fiction becomes scientific fact.

Problem: botulism. Science fiction dreams: to someday produce a container which would preserve food, prevent death. Science-fictional dreamers: Napoleon and his technicians. Dream become fact: the invention of the Tin Can. Outcome: millions alive today who would have otherwise writhed and died.

So, it seems, we are all science-fictional children dreaming ourselves into new ways of survival. We are the reliquaries of all time. Instead of putting saints' bones by in crystal and gold jars, to be touched by the faithful in the following centuries, we put by voices and faces, dreams and impossible dreams on tape, on records, in books, on TV, in films. Man the problem solver is that only because he is the Idea Keeper. Only by finding technological ways to save time, keep time, learn from time, and grow into solutions, have we survived into and through this age toward even better ones. Are we polluted? We can unpollute ourselves. Are we crowded? We can de-mob ourselves. Are we alone? Are we sick? The hospitals of the world are better places since TV came to visit, hold hands, take away half the curse of illness and isolation.

Do we want the stars? We can have them. Can we borrow cups of fire from the sun? We can and must and light the world.

Everywhere we look: problems. Everywhere we further deeply look: solutions. The children of men, the children of time, how can they *not* be fascinated with these challenges? Thus: science fiction and its recent history.

On top of which, as mentioned earlier on, the young people have tossed bombs into your nearest corner art gallery, your downtown art museum.

They have walked through the halls and dozed off at the modern scene as represented by sixty-odd years of abstraction super-abstracting itself until it vanished up its own backside. Empty canvases. Empty minds.

No concepts. Sometimes no color. No ideas that would interest a performing flea at a dog circus.

"Enough!" cried the children. "Let there be fantasy. Let there be science-fiction light."

Let illustration be reborn.

Let the Pre-Raphaelites re-clone themselves and proliferate!

And it was so.

And because the children of the Space Age, and the sons and daughters of Tolkien wanted their fictional dreams sketched and painted in illustrative terms, the ancient art of story-telling, as acted out by your caveman or your Fra Angelico or your Dante Gabriel Rossetti was re-invented as yet the second giant pyramid turned end for end, and education ran from the base into the apex, and the old order was reversed.

Hence your Double Revolution in reading, in teaching Literature and pictorial Art.

Hence, by osmosis, the Industrial Revolution and the Electronic and Space Ages have finally seeped into the blood, bone, marrow, heart, flesh and mind of the young, who as teachers teach us what we should have known all along.

That Truth again: the History of Ideas, which is all that science fiction ever has been. Ideas birthing themselves into fact, dying, only to reinvent new dreams and ideas to be reborn in yet more fascinating shapes and forms, some of them permanent, all of them promising Survival.

I hope we will not get too serious here, for seriousness is the Red Death if we let it move too freely amongst us. Its freedom is our prison and our defeat and death. A good idea should worry us like a dog. We should not, in turn, worry it into the grave, smother it with intellect, pontificate it into snoozing, kill it with the death of a thousand analytical slices.

Let us remain childlike and not childish in our 20-20 vision, borrowing such telescopes, rockets, or magic carpets as may be needed to hurry us along to miracles of physics as well as dream.

The Double Revolution continues. And there are more, invisible, revolutions to come. There will always be problems. Thank God for that. And solutions. Thank God for that. And tomorrow mornings in which to seek them. Praise Allah and fill the libraries and art galleries of the world with Martians, elves, goblins, astronauts, and librarians and teachers on Alpha Centauri who are busy telling the kids not to read science fiction or fantasy: "It'll turn your brains to mush!"

And then from the halls of my Museum of Robots, in the long dusk, let Plato have the last word from the midst of his electro-machine-computerized Republic:

"Go, children. Run and read. Read and run. Show and tell. Spin another pyramid on its nose. Turn another world upside-down. Knock the soot off my brain. Repaint the Sistine Chapel inside my skull. Laugh and think. Dream and learn and build."

"Run, boys! Run, girls! Run!"

And with such good advice, the kids will run.

And the Republic will be saved.

1980

THE SECRET MIND

〜〜〜 I had never wanted to go to Ireland in my life.

Yet here was John Huston on the telephone asking me to his hotel for a drink. Later that afternoon, drinks in hand, Huston eyed me carefully and said, "How would you like to live in Ireland and write *Moby Dick* for the screen?"

And suddenly we were off after the White Whale; myself, the wife, and two daughters.

It took me seven months to track, catch, and throw the Whale flukes out.

From October to April I lived in a country where I did not want to be.

I thought that I saw nothing, heard nothing, felt nothing of Ireland. The Church was deplorable. The weather was dreadful. The poverty was inadmissible. I would have none of it. Besides, there was this Big Fish. . . .

I did not count on my subconscious tripping me up. In the middle of all the threadbare dampness, while trying to beach Leviathan with my typewriter, my antennae were noticing the people. Not that my wide-awake self, conscious and afoot, did not notice them, like and admire and have some for friends, and see them often, no. But the overall thing, pervasive, was the poorness and the rain and feeling sorry for myself in a sorry land.

With the Beast rendered down into oil and delivered to the cameras, I fled Ireland, positive I had learned naught save how to dread storms, fogs, and the penny-beggar streets of Dublin and Kilcock.

But the subliminal eye is shrewd. While I lamented my hard work and my inability, every other day, to feel as much like Herman Melville as I wished, my interior self kept alert, snuffed deep, listened long, watched close, and filed Ireland and its people for other times when I might relax and let them teem forth to my own surprise.

I came home via Sicily and Italy where I had baked myself free of the Irish winter, assuring one and all, "I'll write nothing ever about the Connemara Lightfoots and the Donnybrook Gazelles."

I should have remembered my experience with Mexico, many years before, where I had encountered not rain and poverty, but sun and poverty, and come away panicked by a weather of mortality and the terrible sweet smell when the Mexicans exhaled death. I had at last written some fine nightmares out of that.

Even so, I insisted, Eire was dead, the wake over, her people would never haunt me.

Several years passed.

Then one rainy afternoon Mike (whose real name is Nick), the taxi-driver, came to sit just out of sight in my mind. He nudged me gently and dared to remind me of our journeys together across the bogs, along the Liffey, and him talking and wheeling his old iron car slow through the mist night after night, driving me home to the Royal Hibernian Hotel, the one man I knew best in all the wild green country, from dozens of scores of Dark Journeys.

"Tell the truth about me," Mike said. "Just put it down the way it was."

And suddenly I had a short story and a play. And the story is true and the play is true. It happened like that. It could have happened no other way.

Well, the story we understand, but why, after all these years, did I turn to the stage? It was not a turn, but a return.

I acted on the amateur stage, and radio, as a boy. I wrote plays as a young man. These plays, unproduced, were so bad that I promised myself never to write again for the stage until late in life, after I'd learned to write all the other ways first and best. Simultaneously, I gave up acting because I dreaded the competitive politics actors must play in order to work. Besides: the short story, the novel, called. I answered. I plunged into writing. Years passed. I went to hundreds of plays. I loved them. But still

I held off from ever writing Act I, Scene I, again. Then came *Moby Dick*, a while to brood over it, and suddenly here was Mike, my taxi-driver, rummaging my soul, lifting up tidbits of adventure from a few years before near the Hill of Tara or inland at the autumn changing of leaves in Killeshandra. My old love of the theatre with a final shove pushed me over.

But, also pushing and shoving with free and unexpected gifts, came a mob of letter-writing strangers. Some eight or nine years back I began receiving notes that ran as follows:

Sir: Last night, in bed, I told your story "The Fog Horn," to my wife.

Or:

Sir: I am fifteen years old and won the Annual Recitation Prize at Gurnee Illinois High, having memorized and declaimed your tale, "A Sound of Thunder."

Or:

Dear Mr. B.: We are pleased to report our seven-man semi-staged reading of your novel *Fahrenheit 451* was greeted warmly by 2,000 English teachers at our conference last night.

In a seven-year period, dozens of my stories were read, declaimed, recited and dramatized by grade school, high school and college amateurs all across the country. The letters piled up. Finally, they toppled and fell on me. I turned to my wife and said,

"Everyone except me is having fun adapting me! How come?!"

It was, then, the reverse of the old tale. Instead of crying out that the emperor is naked, these people were saying, unmistakably, that an English flunk-out from Los Angeles High School was fully clothed, and too thick to see it!

I began, then, to write plays.

One final thing jolted me back toward the stage. In the last five years I have borrowed or bought a good many European and American Idea Plays to read; I have watched the Absurd and the More-Than-Absurd Theatre. In the aggregate I could not help but judge the plays as frail exercises, more often than not half-witted, but above all lacking in the prime requisites of imagination and ability.

It is only fair, given this flat opinion, I should now put my own head on the chopping-block. You may, if you wish, be my executioners.

This is not so unusual. Literary history is filled with writers who, rightly or wrongly, felt they could tidy up, improve upon, or revolutionize a given field. So, many of us plunge forward where angels leave no dustprint.

Having dared once, exuberant, I dared again. When Mike vaulted from my machine, others unbidden followed.

And the more that swarmed, the more jostled to fill the spaces.

I suddenly saw that I knew more of the minglings and commotions of the Irish than I could disentangle in a month or a year of writing and unraveling them forth. Inadvertently, I found myself blessing the secret mind, and winnowing a vast interior post-office, calling nights, towns, weathers, beasts, bicycles, churches, cinemas, and ritual marches and flights by name.

Mike had started me at an amble; I broke into a trot, which was before long a full sprint.

The stories, the plays, were born in a yelping litter. I had but to get out of their way.

Now done, and busy with other plays about science-fiction machineries, do I have an after-the-fact theory to fit playwriting?

Yes.

For only after, can one nail down, examine, explain.

To try to know beforehand is to freeze and kill.

Self-consciousness is the enemy of all art, be it acting, writing, painting, or living itself, which is the greatest art of all.

Here's how my theory goes. We writers are up to the following:

We build tensions toward laughter, then give permission, and laughter comes.

We build tensions toward sorrow, and at last say cry, and hope to see our audience in tears.

We build tensions toward violence, light the fuse, and run.

We build the strange tensions of love, where so many of the other tensions mix to be modified and transcended, and allow that fruition in the mind of the audience.

We build tensions, especially today, toward sickness and then, if we are good enough, talented enough, observant enough, allow our audiences to be sick.

Each tension seeks its own proper end, release, and relaxation.

No tension, it follows, aesthetically as well as practically, must be built which remains unreleased. Without this, any art ends incomplete, halfway to its goal. And in real life, as we know, the failure to relax a particular tension can lead to madness.

There are seeming exceptions to this, in which novels or plays end at the height of tension, but the release is implied. The audience is asked to go forth into the world and explode an idea. The final action is passed on from creator to reader-viewer whose job it is to finish off the laughter, the tears, the violence, the sexuality, or the sickness.

Not to know this is not to know the essence of creativity, which, at heart, is the essence of man's being.

If I were to advise new writers, if I were to advise the new writer in myself, going into the theatre of the Absurd, the almost-Absurd, the theatre of Ideas, the any-kind-of-theatre-at-all, I would advise like this:

Tell me no pointless jokes.

I will laugh at your refusal to allow me laughter.

Build me no tension toward tears and refuse me my lamentations.

I will go find me better wailing walls.

Do not clench my fists for me and hide the target.

I might strike you, instead.

Above all, sicken me not unless you show me the way to the ship's rail.

For, please understand, if you poison me, I must be sick. It seems to me that many people writing the sick film, the sick novel, the sick play, have forgotten that poison can destroy minds even as it can destroy flesh. Most poison bottles have emetic recipes stamped on the labels. Through neglect, ignorance, or inability, the new intellectual Borgias cram hairballs down our throats and refuse us the convulsion that could make us well. They have forgotten, if they ever knew, the ancient knowledge that only by being truly sick can one regain health. Even beasts know when it is good and proper to throw up. Teach me how to be sick then, in the right time and place, so that I may again walk in the fields and with the wise and smiling dogs know enough to chew sweet grass.

The art aesthetic is all encompassing, there is room in it for every horror, every delight, if the tensions representing these are carried to their furthest perimeters and released in action. I ask for no happy endings. I ask only for proper endings based on proper assessments of energy contained and given detonation.

Where Mexico surprised me with so much darkness at the heart of the noon sun, Ireland surprised me with so much sun swallowed in the heart of the fog to keep one warm. The distant drummer I listened to in Mexico tread me to a funeral march. The drummer in Dublin tread me lightly through the pubs. The plays wanted to be happy plays. I let them write themselves that way, out of their own hungers and needs, their unusual joys, and fine delights.

So I wrote half a dozen plays and will write more about Ireland. Did you know that people meet in great head-on bicycle collisions, and suffer from fearful concussions for years after, all over Eire? They do. I have caught and held them in one act. Did you know that in the cinemas each night just an instant before the Irish National Anthem is due to explode its rhythms, there is a terrible surge and outflux as people fight to escape through the exits so as not to hear the dread music again? It happens. I saw it. I ran with them. Now I have done it as a play, "The Anthem Sprinters." Did you know that the best way to drive at night in the fog across the boggy midlands of Irish country is keeping your lights off and going terribly fast is better? I have written that. Is it the blood of an Irishman that moves his tongue to beauty, or the whiskey that he pours in to move his blood to move his tongue and tell poems and declaim with harps? I do not know. I ask my secret self which tells me back. Wise man, I listen.

So, thinking myself bankrupt, ignorant, unnoticing, I wind up with one-act plays, a three-act play, essays, poems, and a novel about Ireland. I was rich and didn't know it. We all are rich and ignore the buried fact of accumulated wisdom.

So again and again my stories and my plays teach me, remind me, that I must never doubt myself, my gut, my ganglion, or my Ouija subconscious again.

From now on I hope always to stay alert, to educate myself as best I can. But, lacking this, in future I will relaxedly turn back to my secret mind to see what it has observed when I thought I was sitting this one out.

We never sit anything out.

We are cups, constantly and quietly being filled.

The trick is, knowing how to tip ourselves over and let the beautiful stuff out.

MY THEATRE OF IDEAS

The time, indeed, is theatrical. It is full of craziness, wildness, brilliance, inventiveness; it both exhilarates and depresses. It says either too much or too little.

And one thing is constant through all the instances cited above.

Ideas.

Ideas are on the march.

For the first time in the long and plaguesome

history of man, ideas do not merely exist on paper, as philosophies in books do.

Today's ideas are blueprinted, mocked-up, engineered, electrified, wound-tight and set loose to rev men up or run men down.

All this being true, how rare the motion picture, the novel, the poem, the story, the painting, or the play which deals with the greatest problem of our time, man and his fabulous tools, man and his mechanical children, man and his amoral robots which lead him, strangely and inexplicably, into immorality.

I intend my plays to be first entertaining and grand fun that will stimulate, provoke, terrify, and, one hopes, amuse. This, I think, is important, to tell a good story, to write the passions well, on to the end. Let the residue come when the plays are over and the crowd goes home. Let the audience wake in the night and say, Oh *that's* what he's up to! Or the next day cry, He means *us!* He means *now! Our* world, *our* problems, *our* delights and *our* despairs!

I do *not* want to be a snobbish lecturer, a grandiloquent do-gooder, or a boring reformer.

I *do* wish to run, seize this greatest time in all the history of man to be alive, stuff my senses with it, eye it, touch it, listen to it, smell it, taste it, and hope that others will run with me, pursuing and pursued by ideas and ideas-made machines.

I have been stopped once too often by policemen at

night who ask me what I am *doing,* walking on the sidewalk.

I have written a play called "The Pedestrian," laid in the future, about the plight of similar walkers in the cities.

I have witnessed innumerable seances between television sets and rapt, transported, and oblivious children of all ages, and I have written "The Veldt," a play about a wall-to-wall television room in the very near future which becomes the center of all existence to a trapped family.

And I have written a play about a poet-of-the-ordinary, a master of the mediocre, an old man whose greatest feat of memory is to recall how a 1925 Moon or Kissel-Kar or Buick once looked, down to the hub-caps, windshields, dashboards and license plates. A man who can describe the color of every candy wrapper ever purchased, and the design of every package of cigarettes ever smoked.

These plays, these ideas, put in motion now on the stage, I hope will be considered a true product of our time.

1965

ZEN IN THE ART OF

WRITING

I selected the foregoing title, quite obviously, for its shock value. The variety of reactions to it should guarantee me some sort of crowd, if only of curious onlookers, those who come to pity and stay to shout. The old sideshow Medicine Men who traveled about our country used calliope, drum, and Blackfoot Indian, to insure open-mouthed attention. I hope I will be forgiven for using ZEN in much the same way, at least here at the start.

For, in the end, you may discover I'm not joking after all.

But, let us grow serious in stages.

Now while I have you here before my platform, what words shall I whip forth painted in red letters ten feet tall?

WORK.

That's the first one.

RELAXATION.

That's the second. Followed by two final ones:

DON'T THINK!

Well, now, what have these words to do with Zen Buddhism. What do they have to do with writing? With me? But, most especially, with you?

First off, let's take a long look at that faintly repellent word WORK. It is, above all, the word about which your career will revolve for a lifetime. Beginning now you should become not its slave, which is too mean a term, but its partner. Once you are really a co-sharer of existence with your work, that word will lose its repellent aspects.

Let me stop here a moment to ask some questions. Why is it that in a society with a Puritan heritage we have such completely ambivalent feelings about Work? We feel guilty, do we not, if not busy? But we feel somewhat soiled, on the other hand, if we sweat overmuch?

I can only suggest that we often indulge in made work, in false business, to keep from being bored. Or worse still we conceive the idea of working for money. The money becomes the object, the target, the end-all and be-all. Thus work, being important only as a means to that end, degenerates into boredom. Can we wonder then that we hate it so?

Simultaneously, others have fostered the notion among the more self-conscious literary that quill, some parchment, an idle hour in midday, a *soupçon* of ink daintily tapped on paper will suffice, given inspiration's whiff. Said inspiration being, all too often, the latest issue of *The Kenyon Review* or some other literary quarterly. A few words an hour, a few etched paragraphs per day and—*voilà!* we are the Creator! Or better still, Joyce, Kafka, Sartre!

Nothing could be further from true creativity. Nothing could be more destructive than the two attitudes above.

Why?

Because both are a form of lying.

It is a lie to write in such a way as to be rewarded by money in the commercial market.

It is a lie to write in such a way as to be rewarded by fame offered you by some snobbish quasi-literary group in the intellectual gazettes.

Do I have to tell you how filled to the brim the literary quarterlies are with young lads and lasses kidding themselves they are creating when all they are doing is imitating the scrolls and flourishes of Virginia Woolf, William Faulkner or Jack Kerouac?

Do I have to tell you how filled to the brim are our women's magazines and other mass circulation publications with yet other lads and lasses kidding themselves they are creating when they are only imitating Clarence Buddington Kelland, Anya Seton, or Sax Rohmer?

The *avant-garde* liar kids himself he will be remembered for his pedantic lie.

The commercial liar, too, on his own level, kids himself that while he *is* slanting, it is only because the world is tilted; *everyone* walks like that!

Now, I would like to believe that everyone reading this article is not interested in those two forms of lying. Each of you, curious about creativity, wants to make contact with that thing in yourself that is truly original. You want fame and fortune, yes, but only as rewards for work well and truly done. Notoriety and a fat bank balance must come after everything else is finished and done. That means that they cannot even be considered while you are at the typewriter. The man who considers them, lies one of the two ways, to please a tiny audience that can only beat an Idea insensible and then to death, or a large audience that wouldn't know an Idea if it came up and bit them.

We hear a lot about slanting for the commercial market, but not enough about slanting for the literary cliques. Both approaches, in the final analysis, are unhappy ways for a writer to live in this world. No one remembers, no one brings up, no one discusses the slanted story, be it diminuendoed Hemingway or third-time-around Elinor Glyn.

What is the greatest reward a writer can have? Isn't it that day when someone rushes up to you, his face bursting with honesty, his eyes afire with admiration and cries, "That new story of yours was fine, really wonderful!"

Then and only then is writing worthwhile.

Quite suddenly the pomposities of the intellectual fadists fade to dust. Suddenly, the agreeable monies collected from the fat-advertising magazines are unimportant.

The most callous of commercial writers loves that moment.

The most artificial of literary writers lives for that moment.

And God in his wisdom often provides that moment for the most money-grubbing of hacks or the most attention-grabbing of literateurs.

For there comes a time in the day's occupations when old Money Writer falls so in love with an idea that he begins to gallop, steam, pant, rave, and write from the heart, in spite of himself.

So, too, the man with the quill pen is suddenly taken with fevers, gives up purple ink for pure hot perspiration. Then he tatters quills by the dozen and, hours later, emerges ruinous from the bed of creation looking as if he had channeled an avalanche through his house.

Now, you ask, what transpired? What caused these two almost compulsive liars to start telling the truth?

Let me haul out my signs again.

WORK.

It's quite obvious that both men were working.

And work itself, after awhile, takes on a rhythm. The mechanical begins to fall away. The body begins to take over. The guard goes down. What happens then?

RELAXATION.

And then the men are happily following my last advice:

DON'T THINK.

Which results in *more* relaxation and *more* unthinkingness and greater creativity.

Now that I have you thoroughly confused, let me pause to hear your own dismayed cry.

Impossible! you say. How can you work and relax? How can you create and not be a nervous wreck?

It can be done. It is done, every day of every week of every year. Athletes do it. Painters do it. Mountain climbers do it. Zen Buddhists with their little bows and arrows do it.

Even I can do it.

And if even I can do it, as you are probably hissing now, through clenched teeth, *you* can do it, too!

All right, let's line up the signs again. We could put them in any order, really. RELAXATION or DON'T THINK could come first, or simultaneously, followed by WORK.

But, for convenience let's do it this way, with a fourth developmental sign added:

WORK · RELAXATION · DON'T THINK · FURTHER RELAXATION·

Shall we analyze word number one?

WORK·

You *have* been working, haven't you?

Or do you plan some sort of schedule for yourself starting as soon as you put down this article?

What kind of schedule?

Something like this. One-thousand or two-thousand

words every day for the next twenty years. At the start, you might shoot for one short story a week, fifty-two stories a year, for five years. You will have to write and put away or burn a lot of material before you are comfortable in this medium. You might as well start now and get the necessary work done.

For I believe that eventually quantity will make for quality.

How so?

Michelangelo's, da Vinci's, Tintoretto's billion sketches, the quantitative, prepared them for the qualitative, single sketches further down the line, single portraits, single landscapes of incredible control and beauty.

A great surgeon dissects and re-dissects a thousand, ten thousand bodies, tissues, organs, preparing thus by quantity the time when quality will count—with a living creature under his knife.

An athlete may run ten thousand miles in order to prepare for one hundred yards.

Quantity gives experience. From experience alone can quality come.

All arts, big and small, are the elimination of waste motion in favor of the concise declaration.

The artist learns what to leave out.

The surgeon knows how to go directly to the source of trouble, how to avoid wasted time and complications.

The athlete learns how to conserve power and

apply it now here, now there, how to utilize this muscle, rather than that.

Is the writer different? I think not.

His greatest art will often be what he does not say, what he leaves out, his ability to state simply with clear emotion, the way he wants to go.

The artist must work so hard, so long, that a brain develops and lives, all of itself, in his fingers.

So with the surgeon whose hand at last, like the hand of da Vinci, must sketch lifesaving designs on the flesh of man.

So with the athlete whose body at last is educated and becomes, of itself, a mind.

By work, by quantitative experience, man releases himself from obligation to anything but the task at hand.

The artist must not think of the critical rewards or money he will get for painting pictures. He must think of beauty here in this brush ready to flow if he will release it.

The surgeon must not think of his fee, but the life beating under his hands.

The athlete must ignore the crowd and let his body run the race for him.

The writer must let his fingers run out the story of his characters, who, being only human and full of strange dreams and obsessions, are only too glad to run.

Work then, hard work, prepares the way for the first stages of relaxation, when one begins to approach what Orwell might call *Not Think!* As in learning to typewrite, a day comes when the single letters a-s-d-f and j-k-l-; give way to a flow of words.

So we should not look down on work nor look down on the forty-five out of fifty-two stories written in our first year as failures. To fail is to give up. But you are in the midst of a moving process. Nothing fails then. All goes on. Work is done. If good, you learn from it. If bad, you learn even more. Work done and behind you is a lesson to be studied. There is no failure unless one stops. Not to work is to cease, tighten up, become nervous, and therefore destructive of the creative process.

So, you see, we are working not for work's sake, producing not for production's sake. If that were the case, you would be right in throwing up your hands in horror and turning away from me. What we are trying to do is find a way to release the truth that lies in all of us.

Isn't it obvious by now that the more we talk of work, the closer we come to Relaxation.

Tenseness results from not knowing or giving up trying to know. Work, giving us experience, results in new confidence and eventually in relaxation. The type of dynamic relaxation again, as in sculpting, where the sculptor does not consciously have to tell his fingers what to do. The surgeon does not tell his scalpel what to do. Nor does the athlete advise his body. Suddenly, a natural rhythm is achieved. The body thinks for itself.

So again the three signs. Put them together any way you wish. WORK RELAXATION DON'T THINK Once separated out. Now, all three together in a process. For if one works, one finally relaxes and stops thinking. True creation occurs then and only then.

But work, without right thinking, is almost useless. I repeat myself, but, the writer who wants to tap the larger truth in himself must reject the temptations of Joyce or Camus or Tennessee Williams, as exhibited in the literary reviews. He must forget the money waiting for him in mass-circulation. He must ask himself, "What do I *really* think of the world, what do I love, fear, hate?" and begin to pour this on paper.

Then, through the emotions, working steadily, over a long period of time, his writing will clarify; he will relax because he thinks right and he will think even righter because he relaxes. The two will become interchangeable. At last he will begin to see himself. At night, the very phosphorescence of his insides will throw shadows long on the wall. At last the surge, the agreeable blending of work, not thinking and relaxation will be like the blood in one's body, flowing because it has to flow, moving because it must move, from the heart.

What are we trying to uncover in this flow? The one person irreplaceable to the world, of which there is no duplicate. *You*. As there was only one Shakespeare, Molière, Dr. Johnson, so you are that precious com-

modity, the individual man, the man we all democrat-
ically proclaim, but who, so often, gets lost, or loses
himself, in the shuffle.

How does one get lost?

Through incorrect aims, as I have said. Through
wanting literary fame too quickly. From wanting
money too soon. If only we could remember, fame
and money are gifts given us only *after* we have gifted
the world with out best, our lonely, our individual
truths. Now we must build our better mousetrap,
heedless if a path is being beaten to our door.

What do you think of the world? You, the prism,
measure the light of the world; it burns through your
mind to throw a different spectroscopic reading onto
white paper than anyone else anywhere can throw.

Let the world burn through you. Throw the prism
light, white hot, on paper. Make your own individual
spectroscopic reading.

Then, you, a new Element, are discovered, charted,
named!

Then, wonder of wonders, you may even be popular with the literary magazines, and one day, a
solvent citizen, be dazzled and made happy when
someone sincerely cries, "Well done!"

A sense of inferiority, then, in a person, quite often
means true inferiority in a craft through simple lack of
experience. Work then, gain experience, so that you
will be at ease in your writing, as a swimmer buoys
himself in water.

There is only one type of story in the world. Your story. If you write your story it could possibly sell to any magazine.

I have had stories rejected by *Weird Tales* that I turned around and sold to *Harper's*.

I have had stories rejected by *Planet Stories* that I sold to *Mademoiselle*.

Why? Because I have always tried to write my own story. Give it a label if you wish, call it science fiction of fantasy or the mystery or the western. But, at heart, all good stories are the one kind of story, the story written by an individual man from his individual truth. That kind of story can be fitted into any magazine, be it the *Post* or *McCall's*, *Astounding Science-Fiction*, *Harper's Bazaar*, or *The Atlantic*.

I hasten to add here that imitation is natural and necessary to the beginning writer. In the preparatory years, a writer must select that field where he thinks his ideas will develop comfortably. If his nature in any way resembles the Hemingway philosophy, it is correct that he will imitate Hemingway. If Lawrence is his hero, a period of imitating Lawrence will follow. If the westerns of Eugene Manlove Rhodes are an influence, it will show in the writer's work. Work and imitation go together in the process of learning. It is only when imitation outruns its natural function that a man prevents his becoming truly creative. Some writers will take years, some a few months, before they come upon the truly original story in themselves. After millions of words of imitation, when I was twenty-two years old I suddenly made the break-through, relaxed, that is, into originality with a "science-fiction" story that was entirely my "own."

Remember then that picking a field to write in is totally different from slanting within that field. If your great love happens to be the world of the future, it is only right that you spend your energies on science fiction. Your passion will protect you from slanting or imitation beyond the allowable learning-point. No field, fully loved, can be bad for a writer. Only types of self-conscious writing in a field can do great harm.

Why aren't more "creative" stories written and sold in our time, in any time? Mainly, I believe, because many writers don't even know about this way of working which I have discussed here. We are so used to the dichotomy of "literary" as opposed to "commercial" writing that we haven't labeled or considered the Middle Way, the way to the creative process that is best for everyone and most conducive to producing stories that are agreeable to snobs and hacks alike. As usual we have solved our problem, or thought we solved it, by cramming everything in two boxes with two names. Anything that doesn't fit in one box or another doesn't fit anywhere. So long as we continue to do and think this way, our writers will continue to truss and bind themselves. The High Road, the Happy Way, lies between.

Now—are you surprised?—seriously I must suggest that you read ZEN IN THE ART OF ARCHERY · a book by Eugen Herrigel. Here the words, or words like them, WORK, RELAXATION · and DON'T THINK appear in different aspects and different settings.

I knew nothing of Zen until a few weeks ago. What little I know now, since you must be curious as to the reason for my title, is that here again, in the art of archery, long years must pass where one learns simply the act of drawing the bow and fitting the arrow. Then the process, sometimes tedious and nerve-wracking, of preparing to allow the string, the arrow, to release itself. The arrow must fly on its way to a target that must never be considered.

I don't think, after this long article, I have to show you, here, the relationship between archery and the writer's art. I have already warned against thinking on targets.

Instinctively, years ago, I knew the part that Work must play in my life. More than twelve years ago I wrote in ink on my typing board at my right hand the words: DON'T THINK! Can you blame me if, at this late date, I am delighted when I stumble upon verification of my instinct in Herrigel's book on Zen?

The time will come when your characters will write your stories for you, when your emotions, free of literary cant and commercial bias, will blast the page and tell the truth.

Remember: *Plot* is no more than footprints left in the snow *after* your characters have run by on their way to incredible destinations. *Plot* is observed after the fact rather than before. It cannot precede action. It is the chart that remains when an action is through. That is all *Plot* ever should be. It is human desire let run, running, and reaching a goal. It cannot be mechanical. It can only be dynamic.

So, stand aside, forget targets, let the characters, your fingers, body, blood, and heart *do*.

Contemplate not your navel then, but your subconscious with what Wordsworth called "a wise passiveness." You need to go to Zen for the answer to your problems. Zen, like all philosophies, followed but in the tracks of men who learned from instinct what was good for them. Every wood-turner, every sculptor worth his marble, every ballerina, practices what Zen preaches without having heard the word in all their lives.

"It is a wise father that knows his own child," should be paraphrased to "It is a wise writer who knows his own subconscious." And not only knows it but lets it speak of the world as it and it alone has sensed it and shaped it to its own truth.

Schiller advised those who would compose to "Remove the watchers from the gates of intelligence."

Coleridge put it thus: "The streamy nature of association, which thinking curbs and rudders."

Lastly, for additional reading to supplement what I

have said, Aldous Huxley's "The Education of an Amphibian" in his book, *Tomorrow and Tomorrow and Tomorrow.*

And, a really fine book, Dorothea Brande's *Becoming a Writer*, published many years ago, but detailing many of the ways a writer can find out who he is and how to get the stuff of himself out on paper, often through word-association.

Now, have I sounded like a cultist of some sort? A yogi feeding on kumquats, grapenuts and almonds here beneath the banyan tree? Let me assure you I speak of all these things only because they have worked for me for fifty years. And I think they might work for you. The true test is in the doing.

Be pragmatic, then. If you're not happy with the way your writing has gone, you might give my method a try.

If you do, I think you might easily find a new definition for *Work*.

And the word is LOVE.

1973

. . . ON CREATIVITY

GO PANTHER-PAWED WHERE ALL
THE MINED TRUTHS SLEEP

Not smash and grab, but rather find and keep;
Go panther-pawwed where all the mined truths
sleep
To detonate the hidden seeds with stealth
So in your wake a weltering of wealth
Springs up unseen, ignored, and left behind
As you sneak on, pretending to be blind.
On your return along the jungle path you've made
Find all the littered stuffs where you have strayed;
The small truths and the large have surfaced there
Where you stealth-blundered wildly unaware
Or seeming so. And so these mines were mined
In easy game of pace and pounce and find;
But mostly fluid pace, and not too much pounce.
Attention must be paid, but by the ounce.
Mock caring, seem aloof, ignore each mile
And metaphors like cats behind your smile
Each one wound up to purr, each one a pride,
Each one a fine gold beast you've hid inside,
Now summoned forth in harvests from the brake

Turned anteloping elephants that shake
And drum and crack the mind to awe,
To behold beauty yet perceive its flaw.
Then, flaw discovered, like fair beauty's mole,
Haste back to reckon all entire, the Whole.
This done, pretend these wits you do not keep,
Go panther-pawwed where all the mined truths
sleep.

WHAT I DO IS ME—
FOR THAT I CAME
for Gerard Manley Hopkins

What I do is me—for that I came.
What I do is *me!*
For *that* I came into the world!
So said Gerard;
So said that gentle Manley Hopkins.
In his poetry and prose he saw the Fates that chose
Him in genetics, then set him free to find his way
Among the sly electric printings in his blood.
God thumbprints thee! he said.
Within your hour of birth
He touches hand to brow, He whorls and softly
stamps
The ridges and the symbols of His soul above your
eyes!
But in that selfsame hour, full born and shouting
Shocked pronouncements of one's birth,
In mirrored gaze of midwife, mother, doctor
See that Thumbprint fade and fall away in flesh
So, lost, erased, you seek a lifetime's days for it
And dig deep to find the sweet instructions there
Put by when God first circuited and printed thee to

life:

"Go hence! do this! do that! do yet another thing!
This self is yours! Be *it!*"
And what is that?! you cry at hearthing breast,
Is there no rest? No, only journeying to be yourself.
And even as the Birthmark vanishes, in seashell ear
Now fading to a sigh, His last words send you in the
world:
"Not mother, father, grandfather are you.
Be not another. Be the self I signed you in your blood.
I swarm your flesh with you. Seek that.
And, finding, be what no one else can be.
I leave you gifts of Fate most secret; find no other's
Fate,
For if you do, no grave is deep enough for your despair
No country far enough to hide your loss.
I circumnavigate each cell in you
Your merest molecule is right and true.
Look there for destinies indelible and fine
And rare.
Ten thousand futures share your blood each instant;
Each drop of blood a cloned electric twin of you.
In merest wound on hand read replicas of what I
planned
and knew
Before your birth, then hid it in your heart.
No part of you that does not snug and hold and hide
The self that you will be if faith abide.

What you do is thee. For that I gave you birth.
Be that. So be the only you that's truly you on Earth."

Dear Hopkins. Gentle Manley. Rare Gerard. Fine
name.
What we do is *us*. Because of you. For *that* we came.

THE OTHER ME

I do not write—
The other me
Demands emergence constantly.
But if I turn to face him much too swiftly
Then
He sidles back to where and when
He was before
I unknowingly cracked the door
And let him out.
Sometimes a fire-shout beckons him,
He reckons that I need him,
So I do. His task
To tell me who I am behind this mask.
He Phantom is, and I facade
That hides the opera he writes with God,
While I, all blind,
Wait raptureless until his mind
Steals down my arm to wrist, to hand, to
fingertips
And, stealing, find
Such truths as fall from tongues
And burn with sound,
And all of it from secret blood and secret soul on
  secret ground.
With glee
He sidles forth to write, then run and hide
All week until another try at hide-and-seek

In which I do pretend
That teasing him is not my end.
Yet tease I do and feign to look away,
Or else that secret self will hide all day.
I run and play some simple game,
A mindless leap
Which from sleep summons forth
The bright beast, lurking, whose preserves
And gaming ground? My breath,
My blood, my nerves.
But where in all that stuff does he abide?
In all my rampant seekings, where's he hide?
Behind this ear like gum,
That ear like fat?
Where does this mischief boy
Hatrack his hat?
No use. A hermit he was born
And lives, recluse.
There's nothing for it but I join his ruse, his game,
And let him run at will and make my fame.
On which I put my name and steal his stuff,
And all because I sneezed him forth
With sweet creation's snuff.
Did R. B. write that poem, that line, that speech?
No, inner-ape, invisible, did teach.
His reach, clothed in my flesh, stays mystery;
Say not my name.
Praise other me.

TROY

My Troy was there, of course,
Though people said: Not so.
Blind Homer's dead. His ancient myth's
No way to go. Leave off. Don't dig.
But I then rigged some means whereby
To seam my earthen soul
or die.
I *knew* my Troy.
Folks warned this boy it was mere tale
And nothing more.
I bore their warning, with a smile,
While all the while my spade
Was delving Homer's gardened sun and shade.
Gods! Never mind! cried friends: Dumb Homer's
blind!
How *can* he show you ruins that n'er were?
I'm *sure*, I said. He speaks. I hear. I'm *sure*.
Their advice spurned
I dug when all their backs were turned,
For I had learned when I was eight:
Doom was my Fate, they said. The world would end!
That day I panicked, thought it true,
That you and I and they
Would never see the light of the next day—

Yet that day came.
With shame I saw it come, recalled my doubt
And wondered *what* those Doomsters were about?
From that day on I kept a private joy,
And did not let them sense
My buried Troy;
For if they had, what scorns,
Derision, jokes;
I sealed my City deep
From all those folks;
And, growing, dug each day. What did I find
And given as gift by Homer old and Homer blind?
One Troy? No, *ten*!
Ten Troys? No, two times ten! Three dozen!
And each a richer, finer, brighter cousin!
And in my flesh and blood,
And each one true.
So what's this mean?
Go dig the Troy in *you*!

GO NOT WITH RUINS IN YOUR MIND

Go not with ruins in your mind
Or beauty fails; Rome's sun is blind
And catacomb your cold hotel!
Where should-be heaven's could-be hell.
Beware the temblors and the flood
That time hides fast in tourist's blood
And shambles forth from hidden home
At sight of lost-in-ruins Rome.
Think on your joyless blood, take care,
Rome's scattered bricks and bones lie there
In every chromosome and gene
Lie all that was, or might have been.
All architectural tombs and thrones
Are tossed to ruin in your bones.
Time earthquakes there all life that grows
And all your future darkness knows,
Take not these inner ruins to Rome,
A sad man wisely stays at home;
For if your melancholy goes
Where all is lost, then your loss grows
And all the dark that self employs
Will teem—so travel then with joys.
Or else in ruins consummate
A death that waited long and late,

And all the burning towns of blood
Will shake and fall from sane and good,
And you with ruined sight will see
A lost and ruined Rome. And thee?
Cracked statue mended by noon's light
Yet innerscaped with soul's midnight.
So go not traveling with mood
Or lack of sunlight in your blood,
Such traveling has double cost,
When you and empire *both* are lost.
When your mind storm-drains catacomb,
And all seems graveyard rock in Rome—
Tourist, go not.
Stay home.
Stay home!

I DIE, SO DIES THE WORLD

Poor world that does not know its doom, the day I die.
Two hundred million pass within my hour of passing,
I take this continent with me into the grave.
They are most brave, all-innocent, and do not know
That if I sink then they are next to go.
So in the hour of death they Good Times cheer
While I, mad egotist, ring in their Bad New Year.
The lands beyond my land are vast and bright,
Yet I with one sure hand put out their light.
I snuff Alaska, doubt Sun King's France, slit Britain's
    throat,
Promote old Mother Russia out of mind with one fell
    blink,
Shove China off a marble quarry brink,
Knock far Australia down and place its stone,
Kick Japan in my stride. Greece? quickly flown.
I'll make it fly and fall, as will green Eire,
Turned in my sweating dream, I'll Spain despair,
Shoot Goya's children dead, rack Sweden's sons,
Crack flowers and farms and towns with sunset guns.
When my heart stops, the great Ra drowns in sleep,
I bury all the stars in Cosmic Deep.
So, listen, world, be warned, know honest dread.
When I grow sick, that day your blood is dead.

Behave yourself, I'll stick and let you live.
But misbehave, I'll take what now I give.
That is the end and all. Your flags are furled . . .
If I am shot and dropped? So ends your world.

DOING IS BEING

Doing is being.
To *have* done's not enough;
To stuff yourself with doing—*that's* the game.
To name yourself each hour by what's done,
To tabulate your time at sunset's gun
And find yourself in acts
You could not know before the facts
You wooed from secret self, which much needs wooing,
So doing brings it out,
Kills doubt by simply jumping, rushing, running
Forth to be
The new-discovered me.
To *not* do is to die,
Or lie about and lie about the things
You just might do some day.
Away with that!
Tomorrow empty stays
If no man plays it into being
With his motioned way of seeing.
Let your body lead your mind—
Blood the guide dog to the blind;
So then practice and rehearse
To find heart-soul's universe,
Knowing that by moving/seeing
Proves for all time: Doing's being!

WE HAVE OUR ARTS
SO WE WON'T DIE OF TRUTH

Know only Real? Fall dead.
So Nietzsche said.
We have our Arts so we won't die of Truth.
The World is too much with us.
The Flood stays on beyond the Forty Days.
The sheep that graze in yonder fields are wolves.
The clock that ticks inside your head is truly Time
And in the night will bury you.
The children warm in bed at dawn will leave
And take your heart and go to worlds you do not know.
All this being so
We need our Arts to teach us how to breathe
And beat our blood; accept the Devil's neighborhood,
And age and dark and cars that run us down,
And clown with Death's-head in him
Or skull that wears Fool's crown
And jingles blood-rust bells and rattles groans
To earthquake-settle attic bones late nights.
All this, this, this, all this—too much!
It cracks the heart!
And so? Find Art.
Seize brush. Take stance. Do fancy footwork. Dance.

Run race. Try poem. Write play.
Milton does more than drunk God can
To justify Man's way toward Man.
And maundered Melville takes as task
To find the mask beneath the mask.
And homily by Emily D. shows dust-bin Man's
anomaly.
And Shakespeare poisons up Death's dart
And of gravedigging hones an art.
And Poe divining tides of blood
Builds Ark of bone to sail the flood.
Death, then, is painful wisdom tooth;
With Art as forceps, pull that Truth,
And plumb the abyss where it was
Hid deep in dark and Time and Cause.
Though Monarch Worm devours our heart,
With Yorick's mouth cry, "Thanks!" to Art.